THINKING ABOUT EDUCATION SERIES
SECOND EDITION
Jonas F. Soltis, *Editor*

The revised and expanded Second Edition of this series builds on the strengths of the First Edition. Written in a clear and concise style, these books speak directly to preservice and in-service teachers. Each offers useful interpretive categories and thought-provoking insights into daily practice in schools. Numerous case studies provide a needed bridge between theory and practice. Basic philosophical perspectives on teaching, learning, curriculum, ethics, and the relation of school to society are made readily accessible to the reader.

PERSPECTIVES ON LEARNING
D. C. Phillips and Jonas F. Soltis

THE ETHICS OF TEACHING
Kenneth A. Strike and Jonas F. Soltis

CURRICULUM AND AIMS
Decker F. Walker and Jonas F. Soltis

SCHOOL AND SOCIETY
Walter Feinberg and Jonas F. Soltis

APPROACHES TO TEACHING
Gary D. Fenstermacher and Jonas F. Soltis

CURRICULUM
=== AND ===
AIMS

SECOND EDITION

DECKER F. WALKER
Stanford University

JONAS F. SOLTIS
Teachers College, Columbia University

Teachers College, Columbia University
New York and London

Published by Teachers College Press, 1234 Amsterdam Avenue, New York, N.Y. 10027

Copyright © 1992 by Teachers College, Columbia University

First edition published by Teachers College Press in 1986.

Library of Congress Cataloging-in-Publication Data

Walker, Decker F.
   Curriculum and aims / Decker F. Walker, Jonas F. Soltis. — 2nd ed.
     p.   cm. — (Thinking about education series)
   Includes bibliographical references and index.
   ISBN 0-8077-3142-0
    1. Education—United States—Aims and Objectives.   2. Education—
United States—Curricula.   3. Curriculum planning—United States.
I. Soltis, Jonas F.   II. Title.   III. Series.
LA217.2.W35   1992

                                 91-37170

ISBN 0-8077-3142-0

Manufactured in the United States of America

99 98 97 96 95 94   2 3 4 5 6 7 8

Contents

Acknowledgments

We would like to thank a number of individuals who have contributed in many important ways to the production of this book. Gail McCutchan of Ohio State University invited one of the authors to write on the subject of curriculum theory for an American Educational Research Association (AERA) symposium, prompting a way of thinking about the curriculum field that is reflected in the organization of this book. Karl Hostetler of Teachers College served ably as research assistant and jack-of-all trades to the project, doing copy editing, case development, bibliographic research, and offering many useful suggestions. Frances Simon, with her keen skills at word processing, turned many reworked and barely legible drafts into a finished manuscript. Dorothy Brink's tireless effort and efficiency made it possible to complete the work on schedule. Helpful suggestions for cases came from Nimrod Aloni and Tim Counihan. Nancy Soltis caught many manuscript errors in early drafts. Susan Liddicoat of Teachers College Press provided skillful and caring editorial supervision. And finally, for the second edition we are grateful to the reviewers and users of the first edition for their helpful suggestions.

CURRICULUM AND AIMS

Chapter 1

The Teacher and the Curriculum

This is a book about the curriculum and aims of education. In it we want to stimulate your thinking about what teachers teach in school and what purposes are served by schooling. The "curriculum," as we use the term in this book, refers not only to the official list of courses offered by the school—we call that the "official curriculum"—but also to the purposes, content, activities, and organization of the educational program actually created in schools by teachers, students, and administrators.

Working with the curriculum is an integral part of all teachers' daily lives. When teachers and students talk in the classroom about the rules of good conduct on the playground, that is part of the curriculum. When teachers plan their year's work, decide what their goals for the year will be, what content they will cover, how much they will emphasize different topics, and in what sequence they will present them, they are designing curriculum. When students choose elective courses, vote for officers in student government, or join a student organization, they are helping to shape the school's curriculum. When a principal develops a community service program for student volunteers, that becomes part of the school curriculum. When teachers decide to redirect class discussions that have veered from the main point to a relatively unimportant issue, they are making on-the-spot curriculum decisions. When they decide to set aside their plans for a social studies lesson in order to discuss events of current interest, they are exercising their professional judgment to alter earlier curriculum decisions. And when they make up tests and decide how to weight test results and other data on students' achievement in order to assign grades, they are engaged in thinking about the curriculum. In fact, the curriculum and teaching are as inseparable from one another as the skeleton is from the human body.

In our view, the curriculum is not a separate thing written down some-where that teachers may or may not consult. It is the purposes, content, activities, and organization inherent in the educational program of the school and in what teachers offer in their classrooms. Of course, we often talk about the curriculum as if we could write it down, and, indeed, virtually every school has an official written curriculum that describes, sometimes in general terms and sometimes in great detail, the curriculum school leaders have decided should be offered. For the public, a statement of general principles is usually preferred and appropriate. An entire school program may be described in a page or two—a handful of aims, a list of major courses or subjects, and a brief statement of educational philosophy. For the teachers' use, however, curriculum descriptions are usually written out in great detail. This provides teachers with a comprehensive specification of content, purpose, activities, and organization.

However, there is more to the curriculum than its written version, no matter how detailed that version may be. For instance, a discussion of playground rules in one classroom could simply mean that the teacher presents the rules and the penalties for breaking them with a comment such as, "I hope no one in my class breaks any of these rules." Such an action has quite a different purpose from a discussion in another classroom where the teacher asks students what rules they believe are needed and what the penalties should be—and then students vote on the school rules as part of a schoolwide process of democratic student government. Although the content of these two discussions is the same—playground rules—the purposes and learnings are different—giving students fair warning in the first case, and educating them in self-government in the second; thus the curricula in these two instances would be quite different. In this book we invite you to think about the curriculum in this larger and more inclusive sense and to see that much of what you do as a teacher is important curriculum work.

Ambivalent Feelings About Curriculum Work

For most teachers, their engagement with the curriculum produces some of their best days and some of their worst. Teachers who have never taught a particular grade or subject before or who are new to a school system are usually happy to learn what the school's official curriculum is, even if they do not plan to follow it precisely. Teachers who have never tried to teach a certain idea or skill generally welcome the suggestions given in a curriculum guide, even if these suggestions only serve to spark other ideas of their own. When teachers teach topics that can be controversial—religion, sex, politics, history, or evolution, for example—they may welcome the security provided by an official schoolwide or districtwide position on how controversial subjects are to be treated in the classroom. When designing their own curricula, many teachers find much enjoyment in thinking about new ways to teach their favorite subjects and trying these out in their classes. Some teachers also gain professional renewal and growth from participating in curriculum improvement projects with other teachers or with outside consultants. Some teachers develop reputations and even careers as curriculum developers. And every teacher has at one time or another come to school unprepared for the day's lessons and been saved by the curriculum guide.

On the other hand, curriculum work can be a source of frustration: when a teacher presents a lesson just the way it is described in the curriculum guide and it flops; when a teacher must spend precious hours of personal time week in and week out planning classroom activities because the official curriculum is inadequate or nonexistent; when the official curriculum conflicts with a teacher's deeply held beliefs or clashes with a teacher's personal teaching style; when the official curriculum does not meet the needs teachers perceive the students in their classes to have—the material is too easy or difficult, say, or too remote from their lives; when the official curriculum is drastically revised just when a teacher has truly mastered it and become comfortable with it; when the school administration uses the curriculum as an instrument of domination, imposing it rigidly and offering teachers no freedom or leeway to adapt and adjust it; or when reformers propose major changes in a familiar curriculum and a teacher is uncertain whether to support or oppose the change.

Many of the difficulties teachers have with the curriculum can be traced to three issues:

1. Where can teachers find the time and resources to do curriculum work?
2. How can teachers gain the authority to make curriculum decisions?
3. How can teachers determine when a curriculum change is really a change for the better?

We will elaborate on each of these issues briefly.

Finding Time and Resources for Curriculum Work

Among the most vexing practical problems curriculum work poses for teachers is where to find the time and energy to do the work that is needed. A full schedule of classes five days a week together with the planning they require and the grading of tests and homework is a demanding full-time job for all but the most energetic and enterprising individuals. Yet many teachers must work at second jobs and many have families, so spending evening, early morning, or weekend time on unpaid curriculum planning exacts a heavy sacrifice. Also, curriculum work often requires supplies and equipment in order to create the plans and materials to be used by teachers and students. Teachers need money for word processors or typewriters, copying and duplicating of printed materials, making overhead transparencies, buying books, laboratory equipment, and so on, and many teachers have no school budgets for purchasing such materials and no ready access to such equipment.

Obviously, these are not problems a book on curriculum can solve. All we can do with regard to these real and important practical problems is to call them to your attention and alert you to some of the possible ways you can cope with them in your own teaching assignments. Budgeting time regularly for curriculum work is essential; otherwise the insatiable time demands of students, colleagues, and school administrators will consume all available time. Working as a team with others provides colleagues whose expectations often help to motivate continuing allocations of time to curriculum work. Establishing your own routines for reflecting on your teaching effectiveness can make thinking about curriculum an integral part of your daily life as a teacher. Some teachers find ongoing curriculum innovation projects they can join within the district or at a nearby college or university. Some teachers write grant proposals to initiate curriculum projects of their own. Local foundations are sometimes willing to support worthy innovative projects in local schools. Some teachers become skilled at organizing students and parents to raise funds for materials and equipment. Time and resources for curriculum work can be made issues in contract negotiations between teachers' organizations and the school system. The availability of time and resources for curriculum work is often a factor in a teacher's decision to work for a particular school or school system. Some teachers are able to negotiate unique positions within the district that call for some fraction of their time to be spent in curriculum work and the remainder in classroom teaching. As a teacher, you will need to find strategies that work for you in your local situation for supporting your own curriculum work.

Who Has the Authority to Make Curriculum Decisions?

The most serious institutional problem associated with curriculum work is the issue of who has and should have the authority to make curriculum decisions.

Beginning teachers are usually content to follow curriculum plans prepared by others. They concentrate on transforming those plans into activities that work for them in their classrooms. As teachers gain experience, though, their confidence in their own judgment about curriculum matters grows, and they want to take on a larger role—perhaps to serve on school or district committees to draw up the official curriculum, or to work with a publisher or curriculum project to prepare curriculum materials, and almost certainly to assume control of the curriculum in their own classrooms. At this point teachers confront a truth that many find unpleasant: in public schools in the United States even the most experienced teachers have no generally recognized right, legal or moral, to control the curriculum of their own classrooms. Nor can teachers collectively control the curriculum of their subject or grade. Rather, each of the fifty states has the legal right to set the curriculum of public schools in their state. Most states have traditionally delegated authority over the curriculum to local school systems. Called by various names—districts, boards, townships, counties—these local school systems are political bodies ultimately responsible through their governing boards to local citizens. Only when the curriculum directives of the local school system infringe on a teacher's individual liberties, such as freedom of speech, do they run afoul of the Constitution. But a teacher's freedom to speak any thought as a citizen does not extend to the freedom to present any thought to students in a publicly supported school they may be required by law to attend.

In practice, however, many teachers have virtually a free hand in trying out innovative curriculum plans in their classroom because their school and community leaders trust and support them. But even those teachers who take the most active roles in shaping their own curriculum in systems with strong central control of the school curriculum seldom receive a direct order to conform to the official written curriculum. Rather, when they deviate from it they feel doubt and uncertainty; they may also feel uneasy about whether they have an obligation to inform colleagues and administrators about their deviations, and, when they do, they may receive what they feel are disapproving looks or even open criticism or official reprimands. For innovative teachers in conflict with the official curriculum, the experience is usually a chronic, nagging inhibition rather than a direct confrontation. Even when the reins of power are light, teachers can never afford to lose sight of the fact that their authority in curriculum matters is limited by that of the school system.

Furthermore, students, parents, and the public have rights in curriculum matters, too. In democratic institutions power normally must be shared with other interested parties. Parents have expectations about their children's learning that they try to get schools to meet. Universities and employers set entrance standards that secondary school teachers are pressured to help their students meet. Secondary schools set standards they hope elementary and middle schools will meet. Students themselves exercise some control over the classroom curriculum by giving and withholding their cooperation and by electing certain courses and not others. State legislatures pass laws prescribing certain curriculum offerings for all students. Many states have statewide examinations covering material determined by state agencies to be important for all students to learn. Pressures from these other interested parties ensure that teachers would not have a free hand in curriculum matters even if the law gave them the legal authority to do so.

It should be clear, then, that the curriculum is inherently a social creation, a collective design. Those in positions of official authority in curriculum matters cannot simply implement their own ideas. They have a moral and professional responsibility to consider and respond to the views and interests of all the interested parties. Teachers are the focus of many types of pressure in curriculum matters, as are officials in the local school system, and each teacher needs to develop ways to cope with the resulting tensions between personal ideals and public responsibilities.

In this book we can help you think about the issues of authority and conflicting political interests in curriculum making. To start, it may be enough to suggest some practical strategies for coping with such issues in situations in which you may find yourself. You will need to discover the limits of your authority in your particular teaching position. You can do this by reading official policy statements, but do not expect all the answers you seek to be written down anywhere. Ask both the officials responsible for curriculum in your school—principals, supervisors, curriculum coordinators, and so forth—and experienced colleagues about the freedoms and responsibilities teachers have in curriculum matters in your school. Often practice does not conform to official policy. Listen to stories people tell about teachers who achieved great honor by curriculum work as well as stories about teachers who got into trouble for their curriculum activities. These stories tell indirectly about norms, standards, and values that will figure in the thinking of those in power in your school. Find out how authority over curriculum decisions is shared among interested parties in your school, and work out ways to foster constructive collaboration yourself. Truly professional teachers will do more than follow precedents. They will also assume responsibility for improving the ways the school has devised for sharing curriculum authority.

When Is a Curriculum Change a Change for the Better?

Most of the time teachers rely on their hunches and feelings to tell them if a new curriculum seems promising enough to consider as a replacement for or addition to their own classroom curriculum. Suppose a school system offers a workshop on discipline-based art education for all its 100 or so elementary teachers. The speaker claims that it is possible to teach even young children about the basic ideas of art history, art criticism, and aesthetics while also having them create works of art. The speaker shows videotapes of classrooms where teachers are carrying out discipline-based lessons in art and explains why some experts think children would be better off learning a more balanced and well-rounded view of art rather than simply learning how to use art techniques.

Some teachers may feel that this workshop has opened their eyes to a whole new world of art teaching and learning that they find personally satisfying and that they know in their inmost hearts would be better for their children than the art curriculum they are presently offering. Call it gut feeling or professional judgment—these teachers *know* that this new curriculum is better than their present one.

Other teachers, however, may leave the same workshop feeling upset. They may be convinced that discipline-based art education is a perversion of art, an attempt to make it like the other academic subjects, to reduce it to reading, writing, and verbal knowledge. They may leave the workshop equally convinced that a discipline-based art curriculum would be a terrible idea for their students.

What should be done when teachers disagree about the merits of a curriculum? Should the decision be left to the duly constituted school authorities? Should hearings be held to air the contending views? Should a vote be taken? Should experts be called in? Is there some form of reasoning, problem-solving, or critical thinking that will reveal the correct judgment? Can someone do research that will show which curriculum is the best?

We need to think about what kind of question we are asking when we ask whether a curriculum is good or bad, or better or worse than another. Clearly we are not asking a simple factual question, like what is the capital of South Dakota or how much is two plus two. Are we merely asking, then, whether some people like one curriculum more than another? That hardly seems plausible, either. That would make curriculum choices a popularity contest or just a question of individual preference or fashion. Maybe we are asking about the truth and falsity of curriculum decisions in an academic sense. Can curricula be shown to be false the way scientific theories can be shown to be false by marshaling evidence and arguments against them?

Scholars generally agree that it is not possible, except in some very special cases, to show that a curriculum is false or incorrect. It may be based on a false or incorrect assumption—about learning, say, or about the effectiveness of a particular way of presenting a topic. Showing that a curriculum is based on a false assumption would surely count against it and might cause its advocates to revise it or its rationale so as to avoid dependence on the false assumption. But it might still have many excellent features and, on balance, be an admirable curriculum. Seldom can any complex set of ideas about what should be learned by humans be shown to be completely false; usually the worst that happens is that contending parties offer arguments for and against the ideas and experts disagree about their overall validity, on balance, in light of all these arguments.

Similarly, one can seldom show to the satisfaction of all people of goodwill that a particular curriculum is morally wrong or morally inferior to another. A curriculum could be judged to be morally bad relative to generally accepted moral standards—the educational program of the Hitler Youth organization in the 1930s, for example—but in the vast majority of cases curricula are *prima facie* acceptable or even praiseworthy given the desirable aims they seek to achieve. The value judgments people make when disagreeing about a curriculum are subtle ones that usually turn out to be complex and arguable. Is it better, for example, for art to be taught as a form of creative expression rather than as an academic discipline? From one point of view, yes; from another, no. In some situations, yes—when art is used as part of psychological therapy, for instance; in other situations, no—when helping students understand the role art plays and has played in various cultures, for instance. Value judgments about curriculum questions usually depend not on moral principles like the Golden Rule, the Ten Commandments, or the United Nations Declaration of Human Rights that are nearly universally accepted, but on more arguable value assumptions and perspectives. This does not mean that people feel less deeply about the moral acceptability of curriculum issues; but it does mean that it is more difficult to resolve these issues by appealing to generally accepted principles.

Most often what people mean when they refer to goodness in a curriculum is something like its serviceableness for a certain range of purposes in a certain range of contexts. This is what we mean when we speak of a good clothes dryer or home computer. We mean that it rates highly on the many criteria appropriate to judging the performance and usefulness of such a thing in the context in which we expect to use it. The criteria and standards appropriate for judging a commercial clothes dryer or a business computer may differ from those appropriate for judging similar appliances for use in the home, and the needs of sophisticated users may differ from those of beginners.

When people wonder whether it is better to teach reading using a curriculum consisting largely of exercises graded in difficulty or to teach it by having students write and read their own stories, the answer will depend on which criteria of success they are considering. For example, they could look for reading speed, fluency, size of vocabulary, ability to comprehend typical samples of writing, willingness to read voluntarily, or the cultivation of an appreciation for fine literature. The answer also depends on what contexts they are thinking of—for example, preparation for future studies, for vocational competence, for citizenship, or as a means for attaining students' full human potential. Only rarely will one curriculum be superior to another on every relevant criterion in all contexts, and so there is always room for differences in judgment about the relative merits of the two curricula.

Judgments about the quality of a curriculum depend both on the ideas, values, and points of view people bring to the judgment process and on the details of the situation in which the curriculum is to be used. The best curriculum for highly motivated, academically able, college-bound high school students may not also be the best curriculum for musically, athletically, on artistically talented students who are not interested in academics but are highly motivated in their chosen activities. The curriculum that looks best from the viewpoint of one committed to reducing social inequities as the first priority may not look best from the viewpoint of one committed to fostering the highest expressions of cultural excellence.

We can summarize our position by saying that judgments about the merits of curriculum are many-valued, multifaceted, context-dependent, and relative to larger social, philosophical, and educational viewpoints. To ignore these complexities and just trust one's gut feeling denies the possibility of using one's intellect to guide one's decisions. It also cuts one off from dialogue with others who may have good reasons for reaching a different judgment. And it forecloses opportunities for learning from them and for deepening and correcting one's judgment. It would be better to examine one's reasons for the choices and to discuss one's differences with others in an effort to reach a generally defensible judgment based on the widest range of considerations from a more broadly informed viewpoint. We speak of this as a *fully and fairly considered judgment*. While we cannot demonstrate that a curriculum is correct or true, whatever that might mean, we can still aspire to the goal of reaching the most fully and fairly considered judgment possible under the circumstances we face. The main purpose of this book is to prepare you to consider your own curriculum judgments thoroughly and fairly.

Preparing for Curriculum Work

Teachers can prepare themselves for the challenging demands of curriculum work in several ways: by obtaining practical experience with curriculum work in various institutional settings; by mastering certain methods and procedures; and by acquiring knowledge of fundamental ideas and viewpoints that have guided and continue to guide most curriculum decisions. Reading this book should acquaint you with a number of basic ideas and viewpoints on curriculum that will give you a background for interpreting many practical experiences you have had or may soon have.

The next chapter presents some of the most influential and historically persistent viewpoints on the aims of education by Plato, Rousseau, Dewey, and various twentieth-century progressives and traditionalists. We will encourage you to think about how these viewpoints color contemporary curriculum decisions and how they could and should enter into your own curriculum work.

Chapter 3 invites you to think about and discuss with your peers what should be the purpose, content, and organization of general education—the common education for all. In doing this you should become aware of the different stances that have been taken on this issue and be moved to consider how to go about making good curriculum decisions on this general level. Whatever you teach contributes in some way to the general education of students. By being aware of different ideas about general education and about the ways your teaching of your subject may contribute, you will become a more informed, more professional teacher, and better able to collaborate with others in making curriculum decisions.

In chapter 4 we examine some ideas that provide us with the basic concepts and terms for thinking and talking clearly about particular curricular ideas such as knowledge, experience, instruction, and subjects. Various methods for designing curricula are considered in chapter 5. Then in chapter 6, we step back to get some perspective with the help of some of the contemporary scholars who study actual curricula of the past and present. They will help us understand the current forms that curricula take and raise important questions about their function and desirability.

Chapter 7 places all these ideas in the larger political context in which the working consensus necessary to maintain a curriculum is hard to come by. How do we as a society find a balance among the contending viewpoints and proposals? How do you as a teacher fulfill your obligations to others and maintain your integrity and that of your curriculum? We will offer some insights into this process and suggest a way to proceed.

The last chapter provides a number of dramatic opportunities for you and your fellow students to engage more fully in thinking about curriculum and aims. In this chapter, debates and case studies put some of the ideas and issues dealt with in the main body of the text in a form that requires discussions and resolution. We recommend consideration of specific cases and debates to be read and discussed at the end of each chapter. Using them will help you bring theoretical considerations directly into the resolution of practical problems. We urge you to mix your reading of the text with thinking about these realistic cases and debates. To start, try the case "Curriculum Change," in chapter 8, before you go on. Finally, an annotated bibliography invites you to read and think beyond the elementary treatment of curriculum topics in the text.

This book is a primer, a start at recognizing and thinking about a basic and important part of the world that a practicing teacher works in. As a teacher studying education you will come to see that this kind of thinking and theorizing about curriculum can be of the greatest value to you in your daily curriculum work. It is a vital part of being a truly professional teacher. It will help to make your practice intelligent, sensitive, responsible, and moral.

Chapter 2

The Aims of Education

It hardly seems necessary to remark that curriculum designs and decisions are guided by our ideas of what education should aim at. But what are the aims of education, and where do they come from? How do aims relate to practice, and must a teacher have an aim to carry out the everyday activities of classroom teaching?

Before we try to answer these questions, let us consider a fanciful situation in order to throw some light on the nature of educational aims. Imagine you have been granted three wishes by a genie in a bottle—a genie who has put some restrictions on your wishes. They cannot be wishes for something for you *personally*. The genie will not grant you a sports car or a million dollars or the love of that person you have been dying to go out with for the past six weeks.

The wishes must be for good things for all people, such as good health or a clean environment. What comes to mind? Happiness? Peace? No poverty? One more restriction, then. Your wishes must be for something desirable for people in general *that is only possible for them to have because of something they learn*. People cannot learn to be tall or happy or famous, so you cannot wish for things like that. You could wish them good health, not in the sense that they would never get sick, but in the sense that one can learn to promote one's own health by learning to eat a balanced diet, learning how to exercise properly, learning the early warning signs of serious diseases, and so forth.

In fact, there are a lot of things like good health that curriculum theorists have wished for people—such things as a just society; a harmonious, progressive, democratic nation; the abilities to think critically, act morally, and live responsibly. They also have advocated educating for vocational success, adjustment to life, intellectual discipline, national survival, and a host of other such goals. Envisioning desirable states for individuals and societies that seem approachable or achievable through education is what educational aims are all about. But as John Dewey reminded educators in the early years of this century. "Education as such has no aims, only persons, parents, teachers, etc., have aims, not an abstract idea like education."[1] If you become a teacher, you no doubt will have aims, and others will seek to enlist your support for their aims.

All educators have aims that motivate them and guide what they do. Some aims are remote and intangible; others are more immediate and accessible. In this chapter, we will look at some important aims that have been proposed by educational thinkers. We will also look at the dominant educational debate of this century between traditionalists and progressives and use their thinking about curriculum and aims to highlight some of the features of curriculum that will be addressed in subsequent chapters.

Aims as Ideals

From ancient Greece to the present, the importance of education, of what it does and what it might be structured to do, has been a concern of major Western thinkers. In this section we will briefly discuss the ideas of three philosophers whose ideas about education have had a profound effect on educational thought and practice in Western civilization. In the fourth century B.C., the Greek philosopher Plato (c. 428–328 B.C.) wrote the *Republic*, a major work on government and education aimed at producing the just state. In the eighteenth century, Jean-Jacques Rousseau (1712–1788), the French political philosopher, wrote *Emile*, a treatise on education for freedom. In the twentieth century, America's foremost philosopher, John Dewey (1859–1952), wrote *Democracy and Education*, in which he described a form of education that would serve as the prime fashioner of individual growth and a progressive democratic society.

Before sketching each of these major contributions about curriculum and aims, it is important to see the form this kind of curriculum thought represents. Each of these works views education as the major instrument for producing an ideal state of affairs: a just state, a free individual, or a truly democratic society. As such, they are statements of aims that probably are not fully attainable. Injustice, restrictions on freedom, and imperfect democracy seem to be facts of life, even when we try to overcome them. What good, then, are such ideal aims if we cannot attain them? One answer might be that they point in a direction that is better than their opposites. They proclaim the high value we should place on justice, freedom, and democracy. They also suggest educational practices and procedures that will be consistent with these values and help us achieve at least their partial attainment. Thus they serve as inspirational visions of the Good and stress the role of education in the human quest for the Good Life.

Must an educator have such an ideal aim? R. S. Peters, a contemporary

British philosopher of education, has argued that ideal aims are not necessary, that we can teach without them.[2] He also argued that such high-sounding, unattainable aims are not really objectives to be met as much as they are commitments to certain values and procedures for educating. As you read through our sketches of the educational thought of Plato, Rousseau, and Dewey, ask yourself: Can or do ideal aims play a role in the everyday activities of a teacher, or are they only the high-sounding platitudes of philosophers that are taught in schools of education without much relevance to the real world? Think about it.

For Plato, the ideal aim of education was the just state. The *Republic* begins with Socrates (Plato's alter ego) asking the prior question whose answer is essential before an appropriate plan can be constructed for bringing about the just state. What is justice? What form of social-political life will ensure a just state? Certainly not a society in which the strong rule over the weak in some arbitrary way. Socrates argued that justice requires balance and harmony amongst different groups, with fair treatment of each person according to his nature. This means that, in the ideal city-state, the rulers should be drawn from the most intelligent so that they will be fair and wise in their treatment of all citizens. It means that those who are brave and strong should serve as soldiers in times of threat and that those whose talents lie in the provision of goods and services should devote their lives to these needed tasks in society.

He argued that individuals are, in a way, like society. Individuals thrive when their different parts function in a balanced and harmonious way. The ancient Greeks believed that human beings had bodies that were animated and driven by a three part *psyche*, or soul. Each psyche had an appetitive part, which expressed desires and needs and sought their fulfillment; a spirited part, which put aside unnecessary needs in the interests of self-protection and survival; and a rational part, which rose above both appetite and physical action to provide good judgment through reason.

Keeping these three parts in balance was Plato's ideal of the good person, and balancing the three major functions of the citizenry was his ideal of the just state. Plato realized, however, that individuals were born with different temperaments, capacities, and intellectual endowments. In some, the appetitive part of their psyche was dominant; in others, the spirited part; and in still others, the rational part. Why not, he reasoned, create an educational system that would recognize these individual differences, train the dominant part of a person's psyche, and thereby fulfill the needs of a just society for a balanced order? Those with predominantly appetitive psyches would be educated to satisfy their own needs and the needs of others by becoming farmers, builders, shopkeepers, bakers, winemakers, and the like. The highly spirited would be educated in the

martial arts and become the soldiers and policemen who would unselfish-
ly ensure internal order and courageously protect all against external
threat. And those with predominantly rational psyches would become,
after considerable intellectual and philosophical training, the wise law-
makers, reasonable judges, and supreme leaders of the state. Thus Plato
aimed at an ideal, well-ordered, and well-balanced society through the
education of its members to fill the roles needed for such a society to
function smoothly. Do our schools today sort and train people for the
different vocations needed by society? Is it just to do so? Are we still using
some form of Plato's ideas about educational aims?

Rousseau looked at the corrupt society around him in the eighteenth
century and declared that "all things are good as they come out of the
hands of their creator, but everything degenerates in the hands of
man. . . . Man is not content with anything in its natural state, not even
with his own species. His very offspring must be trained up for him, like a
horse in the menage, and be taught to grow after his own fancy like a tree
in a garden."[3] Thus Rousseau saw the state, society, and parents as having
unrestrained influence on the development and education of individuals,
making them conform to their view of what a socialized and educated
person should be like and robbing individuals of their true identity. In his
major political treatise he wrote, "man is born free and everywhere he is
in chains."[4] The "chains" Rousseau was concerned about were the con-
straints of prevailing social conventions, which mold and shape persons
and keep them from being their own true selves. He reasoned that the
only chance we have to follow our own natures and freely develop as
authentic individual human beings would come if we were freed from the
influence of society in the crucial years of our development. He wrote
Emile, an idealist version of the kind of education he believed was needed
to bring about the development of a free male individual.[5] The early
education of Emile up to the age of twelve was based upon learning from
experience and not from books, learning from nature and not from adults.
The basic tenet of Rousseau's view is that the young child should develop
freely and naturally.

Emile had a tutor, but the tutor was not there to give and hear lessons.
The tutor's role was to allow for Emile's freedom of development and to
help it along without lecturing. One example of how this was done was
Emile's learning that one should not break windows. One day, in a display of anger, Emile broke the window in his room. His tutor neither
chastised him nor made him repair it. In fact, the tutor did nothing. That
night Emile could hardly sleep because he was so cold. Emile decided that
breaking windows when angry was not a very good idea. Many such
"natural lessons" educated Emile. Meanwhile, he was allowed to grow
physically and emotionally without the interference of formal lessons.

After the age of twelve, when Emile had developed his body and senses, his education turned to other areas, including geography and astronomy, but still not to formal lessons. He learned about the earth and the stars directly through experience. With the help of his tutor and still outside the influence of society, Emile learned carpentry and found that he could build and make things useful to himself. The first book given to Emile was *Robinson Crusoe*. From it, he learned to read and shared Crusoe's "building" experiences vicariously. Then, when Emile was about fourteen, the tutor helped him see that all he had become and had learned through the freedom of his own development had enabled him to become a person like others. From this recognition of personhood, Emile then developed a sense of the value of others and deep human feelings of sympathy and responsibility toward them. Now Emile was ready to be educated in history, theology, and philosophy: he was ready to become a free, responsible, educated member of society.

Plato's vision was aimed at using education to produce the balanced, smoothly functioning, just *society*; each individual had his proper place in serving society's needs. Rousseau's vision was of the unique worth of the *individual* and the need for freedom in education to achieve individuality and personhood. Variations on these opposite thematic aims of individual and societal goals for education can be found in every period of our history, even today. In the 1980s numerous national reports on American education were underscoring the importance of high standards and uniform basic curricula in education to ensure our society's political and economic survival in the world. In the 1970s the emphasis in talk about American educational aims had been on providing for individual needs and differences.

Dewey believed that the schools could serve both aims without either submerging individual development in social needs or providing for individual freedom at the expense of social balance and harmony. He thought Plato had been right in recognizing individual differences and the importance of cooperative effort in society, but he criticized Plato for narrowly conceiving of individual differences and talents as being of only three kinds. He believed that education in a democracy had to be more than the education of a class of workers, a class of soldiers, and a class of leaders. He appreciated Rousseau's recognition of the importance of individuality, and of freedom and experience in learning, but criticized Rousseau for not recognizing the importance of the social dimension of learning. Our natural capacities, Dewey argued, are called forth and developed in interaction with others, and this is essential to human growth and development. In his educational writings he tried to reconcile these seemingly irreconcilable aims, one directed at the good of society and the other at the good of the individual.

Democracy, he argued, was not just a form of government; it was a way of people's living and working together that provided for freedom of interaction among groups and for the widest possible sharing of experiences, interests, and values. This, in turn, provided each person with a supportive and nurturing social environment in which to grow and develop as an individual. The ideal school for Dewey was one that took the form of an "embryonic social community," one in which students were encouraged to cooperate and work together and learn from each other as well as from their teachers. In this way, while learning their lessons, they were also learning to be members of a human community.

At the heart of Dewey's ideal view of education was the idea of learning from experience. He believed that freely developing individuals had to learn from their own experiences. He once likened meaningful learning to the kind of learning that an explorer experiences as he moves into uncharted territories. There is the thrill of new vistas, of discovering waterways and mountains, new animal species, and other interesting features. On his return, the explorer produces a map, an abstract sketch of the territory he moved through, which leaves out the experiences he had. Too often, Dewey felt, educators give their students the "map" of some territory of a subject without engaging the students in any of the firsthand experiences that make the map meaningful and useful to them. "Learning by doing" and "learning from experience" became the slogans that progressive educators took from Dewey as they tried to put his ideal aims of education into practice during the first half of the twentieth century.

This idea of learning from experience was very much like Rousseau's. But the freedom provided for students in Dewey's school was not Rousseauian, because it was an immersion in a form of social life conducive to the development of a truly democratic society. Thus Dewey tried to balance these worthwhile but seemingly contradictory aims by providing a rich and meaningful education for individuals in a free but cooperative environment that mirrored an ideal democratic society.

Let us pause and consider the nature of the aims proposed by Plato, Rousseau, and Dewey. Clearly, they differ from such aims as teaching arithmetic or teaching someone how to type. While there are more or less set procedures for teaching typing and arithmetic, the task of attaining a just democratic society made up of free individuals is considerably more complex and problematic. Moreover, learning arithmetic or producing a reasonably proficient typist seem to be achievable goals, whereas achieving a just, free, and perfect democratic society seems to be always out of reach. Peters would say that the real "meat" of the issue of ideal aims lies in the procedures involved, not in attaining the ends posited. He would say that having the aims of justice, freedom, and democracy is really a matter of proceeding in a just, or free, or democratic way as educators. For

Peters such things are not aims to be achieved so much as values to be transmitted through the process of educating in a certain way. What do you think about ideal aims? What function, if any, do they serve in teaching? Before going on, you might want to consider these issues in the case "Freedom and Learning" in chapter 8.

Progressive and Traditional Perspectives on Curriculum

The first half of the twentieth century witnessed a running battle between progressive educators, who saw in the ideas of Dewey and other progressives new ways to think about the curriculum, and the traditionalists, who were sure that the basic curriculum did not need change because it had proven itself essential to the education of individuals who would maintain an intellectually sound and civilized society. Many battles were fought over these opposing views, leaving a profound mark on elementary school practices especially and curriculum theory generally that is still visible today.

In fact, the term *curriculum theory* only came into general use in the United States in the 1920s to describe the writings of perhaps a hundred men and women who were in various ways trying to transform the curriculum of the typical American school. Curriculum revision was one phase of the progressive movement in education. "Progressive education" began to take shape in the United States as early as 1875 and formally ended in the 1950s with the demise of the Progressive Education Society.[6] However, educational reform movements animated by progressive and traditional points of view continue to arise. The British infant school reform of the 1970s and its American counterpart, open education, are recent examples of progressive reforms, while the back-to-basics reforms of the 1980s reflect the traditional point of view.

While we sometimes speak of the progressive education movement as if it were a single entity, progressive educators actually held quite varied views. Some of them were scientists and advocates of a more scientific approach to educational practice. Others were social reformers, primarily interested in improving the lot of the poor and downtrodden. Still others believed in the beauty and goodness of childhood and wanted schools that would not do violence to the child's tender feelings, as they believed the rigidly regimented schools of the day did. And some were pedagogical innovators who had studied the latest theories and practices of the renowned pedagogues of Europe and wanted American schools to become pedagogical pioneers, too.

What the progressives shared was their opposition to prevailing school practices such as rote memorization, drill, stern discipline, and the learning of fixed subject matter defined in adult terms with little relation to the life of the child. However, when they proposed replacements for existing practice, they generated quite a range of ideas. With respect to curriculum revision, for example, some advocated programs built around the arts and self-expression, others championed curricula built around practical training for work and homemaking, and still others urged individualized curricula tailored to the needs of each pupil. Some even expected children to generate their own curriculum based on their own interests and purposes.

Serious debates over curriculum emerged as these reformers tried to convince themselves, one another, and the world that one type of curriculum was better than the others. Those who believed in traditional curriculum practice were challenged by the reformers to explain and defend their views. The result was a rich outpouring of ideas about curriculum and aims, ideas that continue to influence both reformers and traditionalists to this day.

An awareness of the leading ideas of progressivism and the traditional ideas that were the target of progressive reform movements is indispensable to understanding contemporary thinking about the aims of education. Fortunately, the views of many of the most influential writers on curriculum of the progressive era have been collected in one volume, the *Twenty-Sixth Yearbook of the National Society for the Study of Education*, published in 1927.[7] The *Yearbook* was the product of a series of meetings of outstanding academic figures in the curriculum reconstruction movement, then at a peak of activity and centering around the University of Chicago and Teachers College, Columbia University. John Dewey, from whom many of the progressives took their main inspiration, was not a contributor, but the *Yearbook* included a section of selected quotations from his works. Traditional points of view were also represented. In addition, most of the notable school-based curriculum innovators of the day were enlisted as "associated contributors" and prepared statements describing their work in the schools. Thus the ideas expressed in this remarkable volume offer an excellent introduction to the issues that separated the progressive reformers from their traditional opponents. In the next few paragraphs we will only sample its richness.[8] We will do so in the form of a running dialogue abstracted from various articles in the *Yearbook* and assigning them to an imaginary progressive (P) talking to an imaginary traditionalist (T).

P: "Learning of the right kind helps one to live better. In the last analysis we [progressives] concern ourselves about education and learning because we wish our pupils to live fuller and better lives than they otherwise would. It is living that fundamentally concerns us."[9] "What shall

we teach in light of these things? Not the answers to [adult] problems.
. . .No, our procedure must be different."[10]

T: We traditionalists "look on the school as society's agency for guiding
individuals from the immature, relatively unsocial modes of behavior
and thought exhibited in infancy to the mature, more completely socialized forms of thought and behavior exhibited in adult life. [We
have] no hesitation in recognizing present adult society as possessed of
the highest form of organized adaptation that the world knows. [By
means of the traditional curriculum] the mature individual is supplied
with his most significant modes of thought by civilized society."[11]

P: But "the most striking characteristic of the contemporary situation is
the enormous gap between the [traditional] curriculum and the content
of American life. . . . [The] rift between curriculum and society must
be bridged. The content of the school must be constructed out of the
very materials of American life—not from academic relics of Victorian
precedents. The curriculum must bring children to close grip with the
roar and steely clang of industry, with the great integrated structure of
American business, and must prepare them in sympathy and tolerance
to confront the underlying forces of political and economic life. Young
America must awake to the newly emerging culture of industrialism
and she must become articulate. We must discover a sane method by
which useless subject matter can be discarded from the school curriculum and, instead, major problems, institutions, and modes of living
that are of social importance utilized and taught in the lowest school
grades commensurate with the mental abilities and experiences of children."[12]

T: We cannot discard the basic subjects. "The large groups of elementary,
or 'fundamental,' materials seem to be fairly well stabilized. The basic
language-arts and the basic arts of computation and measurement oc-
cupy the place of major importance in universal education. This is true
of the elementary schools of all civilized countries. The degree of universal enlightenment that can be attained through universal literacy is
clearly the first and most fundamental objective of mass education. . . .

"Beyond these basic social arts, there is in most of the civilized
countries a very serious emphasis upon direct moral instruction . . .
[and] civic and health education as ranking close to the fundamental
social arts in importance. . . .

"As subjects of formal instruction, geography and national history
apparently form the backbone of the elementary curriculum on the
side of information as distinguished from skills. This is generally true
of elementary education wherever it has developed beyond the most
rudimentary stages. . . .

"While tradition and imitation have doubtless had some share in giving to these types of groups of materials a place of paramount importance, there can be little doubt that they are also in part the product of an evolutionary process in which, so far as types of species are concerned, the fittest have survived."[13]

P: [Yes.] "Some things, as writing or spelling, can be assigned and we can (within limits) hold children accountable for them, but there are other things that cannot be so assigned. We can make a child stay after school for half an hour, but we cannot make him practice kindness during that time. Nor can we assign honesty as a home lesson for tonight with any hope that one lacking it will have learned it by tomorrow. . . . These things can be practiced only in such life-experiences as in fact call them out. Our curriculum must, then, be the kind to include such life-experiences."[14]

"The pupil has too frequently been required to repeat words, express ideals which he does not understand, and to accept, adopt, and use materials which have been furnished him ready-made and completely organized by the teacher. Learning was thought of as the ability to give back upon demand certain phrases and formulas which had been acquired without adequate understanding of their meaning and content."[15]

"The curriculum should be conceived, therefore, in terms of a succession of experiences and enterprises having a maximum of life-likeness for the learner. The materials of instruction should be selected and organized with a view to giving the learner that development most helpful in meeting and controlling life situations. . . . The method by which the learner works out these experiences, enterprises, and exercises, should be such as calls for maximal self-direction, assumption of responsibility, of exercise of choice in terms of life values."[16]

T: Regarding self-direction, "it is said that pupils should be adopted as the guides to the educational process because the natural unfolding of their interests and desires will lead them forward to that stage of maturity which is to be desired as the end of life. The view here defended is based on a categorical denial of the assumption that the individual unfolds because of inner impulses into a civilized being. Civilization is a social product. It requires cooperation for its maintenance exactly as it required cooperation for its evolution. Even Shakespeare did not create the English language. No child can evolve the English language. Slowly and through great effort and with the help of much patient guidance, the pupil may after long years come to the point where he can share in the social inheritance of his English-speaking environment. His nature will, it is true, unfold in the process of its adoption of the English mode of thought and expression, but this unfolding is not a spontaneous form of growth prompted from within. . . . Knowledge will always have to be systematized and arranged in coherent subjects."[17]

P: But "our present world is a changing world. Never before has change been so persistent or so permeating a factor. Moreover, there is every promise that, rapid as change has been, it will be even more rapid in the future. Our young people face, then, an unknown future. Once education could merely repeat the past. That time has gone. . . . Education must know that we face an unknown and shifting civilization" and our curriculum should reflect this.[18]

This imaginary debate, drawn from real sources, highlights some of the differences between viewpoints regarding curriculum and aims that were passionately believed and argued about not so very long ago. They illustrate how progressive curriculum theory and practices diverge quite sharply from traditional ideas and practices. The contrast is so great and so striking that educators still tend to perceive many new ideas and practices in terms of their similarity to these two extreme positions, just as we perceive political ideas in terms of left and right, liberal and conservative. This categorization does help us to see relationships among a confusing array of ideas, but it can also interfere with our ability to accept an unfamiliar proposal on its own terms. Stereotypes can be dangerous, but in the paragraphs that follow we will try to highlight some of the general features of progressive and traditionalist viewpoints so you can gain a better appreciation of them. As you read them, try to think of things in your own education that might have reflected these positions.

Progressives favor change. They are more impressed with the ways things change than with how they stay the same. To them, the present is decidedly imperfect and must be improved. We should work in the present to make the future better. Traditionalists are suspicious of change. They believe we have struggled through the centuries to develop our knowledge and our culture and that these are too precious to change at the drop of a hat or leave their transmission to the next generation to chance. A better future can only be built on a solid base of past achievements. To a progressive, prevailing ideas and practices reflect the past and thus are likely to be conservative if not regressive.

The progressive sees history as dynamic. The economy, the society, the polity, are constantly changing, and we must learn to bring our ideas and behavior into line with these changes. We need not worry about preserving what is valuable from the past. A tremendous inertia is built into human affairs that more than adequately protects our inheritance. As for the notion of "surviving the test of time," the true progressive regards every day as a new test, independent of all those that have gone before, just as likely to topple the old giant of the forest as the young seedling. The traditionalist treats the past with reverence and respect, as a valuable inheritance that we should learn about, use, add to, and pass on to the next generation.

Progressives align themselves with the young, who are untainted by the prejudices of the past, against the entrenched powers supported by prevailing ideas and practices. Youth is seen as likely to be innocent and good, whereas bias and evil are more likely to arise with age. The traditionalist sees the adult as the mature and wise judge of what the young need to learn. Discipline is required to curb the impetuousness of youth and provide fertile ground for passing on the wisdom of the past.

For the progressive, freedom is more important than discipline or order, since only original exploration can discover the directions we should take toward a better future. Actual experiences of people in the present are a surer guide than the inherited "wisdom" of a past quite different from our present. Experimentation is the test of any idea or action. Traditionalists believe that a study of the academic disciplines provides training for the mind; and both rationality and mastery of the main forms of human knowledge are essential for solving our problems. Our human traditions and institutions are also important, because they bring order into our lives.

Progressives believe that individuals must learn to think for themselves in order to combat the tendency toward authoritarian social control through "prevailing views," which are usually the views favored by those in power, who are, in turn, supported by traditional ideas and practices. Creative individuals with original ideas must be nurtured, for they enable us to adapt intelligently to changing conditions. Furthermore, individuals must be encouraged to act on their ideas, or else they will be ineffectual, governed by entrenched traditions instead of their own experience.

Curriculum Theory

It is important to see in these differences that curriculum theory is something people feel strongly about. The questions dealt with are of more than merely academic interest. Curriculum theory, being closely connected with our views of what is true and important about ourselves and our world, reaches far down into our personal, social, and cultural depths. In deciding what and how to teach our children, we are expressing and thus exposing and risking our identity—personal, social, and cultural. In expressing what we think is true and important, we run the risk that others who disagree may oppose us or that we may come to question our own beliefs. Yet we cannot avoid this risk as educators, because we must act.

Doing nothing about curriculum matters is an action that leads to certain consequences for which we would be responsible in just the same way we would had we acted vigorously.

And so, curriculum theory deals with matters that are likely to be highly charged and of great moment to many people, not just theorists. In this it is unlike most scientific or academic theories, except that in an interesting way it resembles those theories that have most seriously affected humanity's image of itself—Copernicus's heliocentric theory, Darwin's theory of evolution, Marx's theory of economics, and Freud's theory of psychology. Ordinary people have felt themselves to have something at stake in the question of the truth of these theories; they feel the same way about curriculum theories, and for the same reason—these theories touch on matters of great personal significance.

Whether the ideal aims of Plato, Rousseau, or Dewey should be our guides, or whether a progressive or traditionalist stance toward the purposes and processes of education should claim our loyalty, are questions of great weight and cannot be answered easily. They need to be thought about, wrestled with, and seriously considered and debated with others. This way of thinking about curriculum is the most basic of all the ways we will introduce you to in this book. Before going on, you might want to look at the debate "Education for Life" and the case "Workforce School," in chapter 8. In the next chapter we will explore the problem of general education in a democratic society by looking at some answers to the question, What education is the best education for all?

Chapter 3

General Education

What kind of education would best ensure every person's attainment of effective and responsible membership in a democratic society? What kind of education would best prepare each person for any situation they may encounter in life? The person may be dull or brilliant, profound or shallow, rebellious or docile, interested in school or not, rich or poor, female or male, of any political persuasion, with any set of interests, with any aspirations or lack of them. The person may be destined for any walk of life from the humblest to the mightiest, from the active to the contemplative, and for any occupation. This is the problem of general education. It is to find the most appropriate common curriculum and aims to meet these difficult requirements of honoring individuality while also serving the democratic purposes of society.

Every democratic society that attempts to provide some form of universal education for all its members faces this problem. When children are born no one can know what their qualities will be, and, in an open and democratic society, no one can know what way of life they will follow. So the education we provide must prepare all children to become equal participating members in a free society in which they will have a future of open-ended possibilities. This is a much different problem, and a much harder one, from designing a technical or vocational program to prepare a specific type of student for a specific career. It is a problem that all teachers face no matter what subject or grade level they teach. They must answer the question: What general characteristics should an educated person and a democratic citizen have, and how can I foster them in my classroom?

Take a moment now and think about how you would answer the question: What should be the aims of general education? When you have found some answers that you feel comfortable about, compare yours with ours or those of your classmates. Did we come up with similar answers or were the answers quite different? Do not be surprised if you discover differences. There have been numerous debates over the goals and best form for general education in our society.

On our list is the development of such things as individual potential and talents, intellect and critical-thinking skills, general vocational skills needed in all kinds of work, cultural literacy, basic literacy (the 3 Rs), a core of historical, social, and scientific knowledge, the dispositions and values of democratic citizenship, and others.

Some people feel strongly, however, that some of these answers are better than others. For them, general education should concentrate its energies on a single most important goal. For instance, a teacher may be convinced that the best form of general education is one that fosters the greatest development of the unique qualities and talents of each individual student. For this teacher other ideas about general education may seem less significant, flawed, biased, or partial by comparison with the notion of self-development. The teacher may even have entered the profession primarily out of dedication to this ideal. Such a teacher could act on that belief by making as many curriculum decisions as possible in ways that promote this form of general education. For instance, such a teacher could give students every possible opportunity to choose their own goals and content, and could even negotiate separate contracts with each student spelling out the achievements that would be required for that student to earn a particular grade. Such a teacher could approach every curriculum issue with a single-minded criterion: What most promotes individual students' self-development?

If you are such a teacher, you might think that you only need to learn about the one point of view on general education that you are convinced is superior. However, if other interested parties in your school hold different beliefs about general education, your freedom to put your preferred form of general education into practice will probably be limited. You would eventually come into conflict with others—parents, fellow teachers, or school officials—who believe as strongly as you do in some other ideas about general education. As a professional, you need to be able to talk to such people, to understand their point of view, and to enter into a dialogue with them about curriculum issues. So, even if you believe one of these answers to the problem of general education is clearly superior to all others, your duty as a professional requires you to share curricular authority with others who may have different beliefs. How would you reply to other challenging positions? Consider the idea of the importance of teaching the basics.

Teaching the Basics

What studies are so basic as to be required of every student? You would probably agree with the overwhelming majority of people that all students need to read, write, and use numbers for the ordinary purposes of life. Most people believe that literacy is essential in order to function in the daily life of an increasingly complex society, but some people think that electronic media such as television and telephones are making literacy less essential. What do you think? If you are uncertain, how would you try to decrease your uncertainty?

You could also make a strong case that interpersonal relations are basic. The pathologically shy person and the violently aggressive one can only function with the greatest difficulty in a modern society, no matter how literate they may be. Nor can emotionally disturbed children learn effectively. Would you make interpersonal skills part of the basics of your program of general education? If so, how would you go about educating children in interpersonal skills? If not, how would you reply to those parents or teachers in your school who might advocate them as basic?

A convincing case can be made that political and civic education are basic. Preservation of the polity, prevention of internal strife, and the maintenance of an orderly society are clearly prerequisites to any of the other good things we desire from education. Should civic and political education be basic? What about health and physical education? Wellness is a good in itself, and it also enables people to pursue other goods with more energy and vitality. What about the practical economics of budgeting, making wise consumer choices, and the like? What about preparation for a job?

At one time or another, all of these have been considered basic in American public education. On the other hand, each of them has been challenged by critics. If you were inclined to accept all of these items as basic, reflect that you would be open to the charge that your curriculum is cluttered with a hodgepodge of content and your energies divided among conflicting aims. What is truly basic?

Historical Precedents

Let us look at some of the classic attempts in the last hundred years to address the problem of what is basic and what should be the content and aims of general education. In our society general education is provided in elementary schools by offering a single broad and comprehensive curriculum to all. In secondary education, the problem of general education becomes more pronounced. Students are ready for diversification and specialization. For many, high school is the terminus of their formal education, and educators see this as their last chance to complete the task of general education.

In the latter part of the nineteenth century, secondary education in the United States was extremely diverse in type and quality, ranging from demanding private academies that taught Greek, Latin, astronomy, geometry, and other advanced academic subjects to trade schools that taught functional English and manual skills. Leading colleges had expressed concern that high school graduates applying to college were poorly prepared to undertake college work in all the required subjects. They felt that solid academic work in the disciplines was essential not only for entrance to higher education but for the best education of all.

In 1893 the National Education Association (NEA) appointed a committee, later called the Committee of Ten, to help standardize the high school curriculum. The Committee of Ten, made up primarily of college teachers and headmasters of private schools, was chaired by Charles Eliot, then president of Harvard University. This group recommended nationwide adoption of four standard patterns for the high school curriculum—classical, Latin-scientific, modern languages, and English.[1] All four consisted mainly of traditional academic courses, and the Committee recommended that colleges accept any student who had completed any one of these high school curricula as adequately prepared for college work. The Committee of Ten reports were silent about practical and vocational subjects and also did not mention the arts. They went into great detail about classics, science, English, mathematics, and social studies. The reports of the Committee of Ten outlined a pattern of courses that soon became standard. High school education for all became an education in the disciplines. Even today, the college preparatory high school curriculum in most schools strongly resembles the recommendations made by this Committee a hundred years ago.

Twenty-five years after the Committee of Ten reports, the NEA established a new group to examine the high school curriculum, the Commission on the Reorganization of Secondary Education. This group, made up mainly of teachers and principals in public schools, was strongly guided by the ideas of progressive education. Their 1918 report, which came to be referred to as the *Cardinal Principles of Secondary Education*, defined the basics not in terms of what students needed to succeed in college but of what they needed to succeed in life outside the school and of what the society needed all students to learn. The seven Cardinal Principles they stated embody their conception of what should be basic in secondary education. The "main objectives of education" according to the Commission were:

1. Health
2. Command of fundamental processes [reading, writing, arithmetic, oral expression]
3. Worthy home membership
4. Vocation
5. Citizenship

6. Worthy use of leisure
7. Ethical character[2]

The Commission report argued that every school subject should be reexamined and, if necessary, reorganized, so that it contributed to these aims. Any subjects that did not contribute sufficiently should be dropped and replaced with other subjects, topics, or themes of study. In the two or three decades following the Commission's report, American schools engaged in an unprecedented amount of curriculum experimentation. Schools tried curricula organized around projects and around integrated core subjects that combined English and social studies or science and mathematics, and curricula created by students and teachers around their own distinctive needs and interests. The division of secondary education into junior and senior high schools dates from this period, and the Cardinal Principles were an important influence in the establishment within a few decades of the comprehensive high school, offering academic, vocational, and general programs within the same school.

The problem of general education in the United States was not solved, however. In the mid-1940s a committee of the faculty at Harvard put the problem this way in their report entitled *General Education in a Free Society*.

> Taken as a whole, education seeks to do two things: help young persons fulfill the unique, particular function in life which is in them to fulfill, and fit them so far as it can for those common spheres which as citizens and heirs of a joint culture they will share with others. . . . The question therefore has become more and more insistent: what then is the right relationship between specialist training on the one hand, aiming at any one of a thousand different destinies, and education in a common heritage and toward a common citizenship on the other? . . . The ideal is a system which shall be as fair to the fast as to the slow, to the hand-minded as to the book-minded, but which, while meeting the separate needs of each, shall yet foster that fellow feeling between human being and human being which is the deepest root of democracy.[3]

To fashion this feeling, a basic general education was proposed for all, one that would provide each student with exposure to our common heritage through a nonspecialized study of the humanities and the social and natural sciences, while being geared to each student's level of ability.

After describing the problems they perceived in American education at midcentury, the Harvard Committee went on to elaborate the curriculum they believed would accomplish this difficult task of providing adequate specialized, as well as general and common, education for all, given the diversity of student abilities and interests. Not surprisingly, they recommended that half of a student's course work be drawn from general education courses. In high school, that translated into three courses each (or Carnegie units) of English, science, and math, and two of social studies. These were to be taught as general courses for the nonspecialist. Furthermore, these courses, and general education in general, were to be aimed not only at providing some common knowledge base for all future citizens but also at developing certain mental abilities. "These abilities in our opinion are: *to think effectively, to communicate thought, to make relevant judgments, to discriminate among values.*"[4] Finally, all students would be required to specialize, to learn skills appropriate to some vocation. This would allow them to become productive citizens and fully honor their individual talents and skills.

> Our conclusion, then, is that the aim of education should be to prepare an individual to be an expert both in some vocation or art and in the general art of the free citizen. Thus the two kinds of education once given separately to different social classes must be given together for all alike.[5]

The Harvard Report did not solve our problems, however. The period after World War II to the present has been characterized by persistent critiques, reactions, and reforms of general education. Reacting to questions from "Why can't Johnny read?" to "Why do the Japanese outperform us economically?" other national committees and their reports have led to curriculum reforms of many kinds. Today, contemporary problems of general education persist in the symptomatic form of high dropout rates, lower SAT scores, cultural illiteracy, and monoculturalism in the schools of our pluralistic society.

In considering curriculum problems such as these, it is often helpful to reflect on the historical origins of the various views people today put forward about them. For one thing, the study of history can take us out of what may be an overly narrow contemporary perspective by showing us that views other than those most people hold today on these issues have been held on similar issues by others in the past, suggesting that these different views might again be valid if similar circumstances prevailed. For another, realizing the historical circumstances that gave rise to a certain point of view enables us to ask now whether these views continue to be as pertinent to our situation today. Furthermore, it helps to know what our predecessors thought, said, and did and what happened to their initiatives, so that our own decisions can be better informed. Curriculum decisions can be viewed as a continuing dialogue uniting us with our ancestors and with posterity.

Relating School to Life

In arriving at your answer to the question of general education with which we began this chapter, did you consider the need to make the school program relevant to the lives of students? British educator G. H. Bantock has thought deeply about the relation of the formal school program to life outside the school and offers a challenging perspective and set of recommendations from a historical perspective.[6]

According to Bantock, until the coming of industrialization in the nineteenth century, Western civilization supported two cultures, a "high culture" confined to the upper classes and based on the ability to read and write, and a "folk culture" based largely on traditions of oral communication. He argues that the routine of industrialization impoverished the everyday life of working people and undermined folk culture. Work, which had offered innumerable sensory and emotional satisfactions and had furnished the materials for folk art, was transformed into machine-governed routines with far less aesthetic and emotional potential. The efficient, mechanical organization of work replaced the organic, personal, and natural flow of interpersonal interaction prevalent on the farm, in the shop, and in the home.

Universal literacy, fostered by free and compulsory elementary schools in the late nineteenth century, imposed upon the working-class majority of Europeans the rudiments of the high-literacy culture of the upper classes and ruthlessly extirpated the remnants of folk culture. In school, culture meant the culture of the educated minority, "the best that has been thought and said." There was no room for the nonliterate, oral tradition or for the nonliterary arts—dancing, singing, handicrafts, popular performing arts, and the like—that constituted the popular culture of the day.

For children of the working class, the results of this education were alienation from the only living, encompassing culture open to them, along with a failure to induct them fully into the high culture. The bits and scraps of literacy conveyed in the few short years of elementary education were poor preparation for a rewarding, satisfying life in any adult community. The school stood for abstraction and a purely mental life, whereas the authentic traditions from which the children had come were based upon direct contact and immediate participation, upon the senses and the feelings. This school was then and remains today a failure for a substantial proportion of the populace.

Bantock believes that today we have another popular culture, built around the mass media. It is not a folk culture, because it is not created by the folk but rather consumed by them. Yet it is still largely nonliterate and appeals directly to the senses and the feelings. Thus the school is still in the position of offering the remains of a high, literate culture to a population of children whose lives at home are built around a completely different mass culture. "The world implicit in work of the school variety is the stubborn, irreducible real world; that contained in pop culture is one manufactured out of floating emotions and aspirations exploited by clever men who thus feed rather than check the dreams of unreality."[7] This, according to Bantock, is the chief dilemma of education in the twentieth century.

> The culture of people, then, is one which, generally speaking, appeals to the emotions. I have tried to show that, all too often, it is a cheap and tawdry culture, likely to betray one's sense of emotional reality, erecting "images" of no substance between the individual and his attempt to grapple with the real world of relationships, inhibiting true empathy or fostering a debilitating sentimentality. Yet this too has to be said. This culture is enormously appealing, in the emotionally undereducated environment we inhabit. It clearly "gets" young people to an extent that school achieves but rarely.[8]

Bantock argues that no one curriculum could satisfy the needs of both children of the elite, literary culture and children of the popular culture. The traditional literary-historical curriculum is fine for the first group, but the curriculum for children of the lower classes will need to be wholly redesigned. For them, education needs to unite thought and feeling; to use their natural propensities toward direct participation, sensing, and feeling; but to use them to the ultimate end of introducing them to higher, more serious, more refined, and ultimately more truthful and satisfying ways of dealing with reality.

Bantock proposes an elementary school curriculum designed for education of the emotions. The methods and concerns of the arts lie at the heart of this curriculum. Bantock proposes movement education as the starting point. In movement education children both explore space in a disciplined way and learn to express their feelings through movement. For instance, children may be asked to devise a movement sequence that involves their entire body, fills the volume of a cube equal to their height, and expresses defiance. From such starting points, children can develop kinesthetic bases for mathematics and logic as well as prepare themselves for study of narrative, symbol, and other elements of drama and literature. Study of movement and other arts leads naturally into careers in theater, film, and television, and it also provides students with a basis for aesthetic judgment of works in those and other media. Bantock also argues that schools should teach about home and family life and vocational and technical careers, not through academic study alone but beginning as always with direct contact and participation.

Do these ideas of Bantock suggest lines of thought about general education that you overlooked in your first thoughts about the subject? Would you endorse his recommendations? If so, does it bother you that this would be a form of education explicitly divided by class? What are the implications of this for such democratic ideals as social mobility and equality of educational opportunity?

In Search of the Best Curriculum for General Education

As we have seen, thoughtful people have debated the question of general education for centuries, leaving us with a valuable legacy of ideas, proposals, and points of view. We will encounter more of these authors and their ideas throughout this book. It is also apparent that advocates of each position have done their best to demonstrate through careful reasoning and by marshaling evidence that their position is superior to the others. However, even though this debate has clarified the strengths and weaknesses of the various positions, the controversy has not been resolved. This puts teachers in an awkward position in making curriculum decisions. If only someone had been able to determine that one curriculum provided the best preparation for life in an open, democratic, postindustrial society in the twenty-first century, teachers would be able to adopt this curriculum. If only scholars had reached a consensus that one point of view on the best curriculum for general education was superior to other points of view, this would help teachers considerably. But, in fact, careful study seems to lead to the conclusion that most of the classic answers to the question of general education contain at least a germ of truth and therefore cannot be wholly dismissed. This suggests that these different answers reflect inherent differences of values or perspectives that can never be fully resolved.

One of the oldest and still most valuable insights into these differences suggests that opposing positions on curriculum questions often reflect a bias toward one of three *commonplaces* of education: the student, the society, and knowledge (or subject matter, what is to be learned). Some of the positions on general education reflect a student-centered perspective, such as the position of the Commission on the Reorganization of Secondary Education in their seven Cardinal Principles. Others reflect a society-centered perspective, such as Bantock, and still others reflect a subject-centered perspective, such as the Committee of Ten. Each perspective puts one part of the entire educational situation in the foreground, and that inevitably pushes the other parts to the background. Let us look at these three perspectives in more detail.

The subject-centered perspective—that education exists primarily to transmit knowledge to each new generation and prepare them to add to it—is perhaps the oldest idea of general education. Those who take this perspective are likely to support such aims of education as:

Literacy
Command of basic skills
Mastery of basic facts and theories in fundamental subjects
Critical thinking
Problem solving
Good study skills and work habits
Desire to learn

They are likely to oppose aims not closely related to these, such as health, vocational training, character training, acquisition of social skills and graces, and personal or social adjustment. They see these other aims as detracting from the primary function of general education—transmission of knowledge. Proponents of a subject-centered perspective disagree among themselves on which parts of the vast body of knowledge are most important to teach in the limited time available in school, on the priority to be given to transmission of existing knowledge and discovery of new knowledge, and on the most effective means for conveying the knowledge to young people. But they agree that the main aim of general education is to transmit formal knowledge.

That education is an instrument of society is not antithetical to the idea of education as transmission of knowledge—it has generally been assumed that knowledgeable people improve the general welfare of society at large. But many firmly believe that education's responsibility to the society that supports it goes far beyond this. The ancient Greek city-state Sparta, for instance, provides one of the clearest examples of using education to mold people to the needs of the larger society. The Spartan state supervised every aspect of the education of its young people, including forced separation from parents at an early age, compulsory military training, and severe restrictions on every aspect of personal conduct. Its education system was designed to support its military aims. Throughout history many educational systems were established to maintain and improve the welfare of the society that established them, regardless of effects on particular individuals or on the body of formal knowledge. Although those who adopt a society-centered perspective on general education may disagree about what is most needed for the welfare of their society and about the educational means that will most effectively provide it, they agree that the survival and smooth functioning of the society is what education should be about.

The society-centered perspective has played an important part in

American education from the beginning. Creating a sense of national identity separate from Europe was the primary aim of Noah Webster, the dictionary compiler and pioneer author of American schoolbooks. The renowned McGuffey Readers gave a moral purpose to practically everything studied in the early American school. Arithmetic lessons featured problems from everyday life—accounting, surveying, mechanics—to prepare children for the practical problems that would have to be solved if the new nation was to prosper. The spread of the common school and universal compulsory education in the nineteenth century was touted as a way to prevent juvenile delinquency, control crime, and produce a more productive workforce. Early in the twentieth century, progressive educators placed enormous emphasis on the social role of education and fought vigorously against what they saw as a narrow academic focus of the schools. They favored such aims as:

Civic responsibility
Vocational preparation
Development of democratic attitudes
Health
Personal and social adjustment
Ethical values and behavior
Concern for the welfare of others

In recent decades a steady stream of social demands have been put on schools—to Americanize immigrants, counter the threat of totalitarianism and communism, prepare a workforce for an industrialized and then a postindustrial society, prepare for global economic competition, foster integration of racial, economic, and social groups, and so on. The society-centered perspective is clearly still well represented in American education.

Those who view education primarily from the perspective of the individual student, on the other hand, place great importance on individual rights, the development of individual talents, personal fulfillment, the pursuit of happiness, and individual social, economic, and intellectual advancement. Freedom is the rallying cry of this group, and the vision of an education freed from authoritarianism and compulsion, from conformity and rigidity, has captured the imagination of many generations of educational reformers. At the goading of these reformers struggling under the banner of freedom, modern education has shed some of its harshest characteristics. Stern discipline, punishment, and fear have given way to more positive methods involving warmth, kindness, and respect. Externally imposed work and discipline are introduced gradually into school activities that begin as play. Rigid, uncomfortable clothing, seating, and physical arrangements have given way to more informal and pleasant surroundings. Rather than suppressing children's unsocialized impulses, schools now encourage their expression in socially acceptable ways.

In many ways a student-centered perspective is characteristic of education in our age. Those who adopt it tend to favor such aims as:

Self-realization
Self-esteem, emotional stability, mental health
Creative expression
Cultivation of personal talents and interests
Wise use of leisure time
Preparation for contemporary life
Health and safety

Advocates of student-centered aims tend to view academic goals beyond the basic skills needed for living as appropriate for those students whose talents and interests so include them, but not necessarily for all students, especially when the study of academic subjects is not intrinsically motivating and does not contribute to their personal happiness. Student-centered educators resist the idea of imposing socially approved ideas on students, believing that society is there for the benefit of individuals and not the reverse. Schools should help each student realize his or her potential. While they disagree about how this potential is to be identified and what form of education will best nurture its development, they agree that this should be the primary aim of general education.

The Value of Different Perspectives

Perspectives such as these can help teachers make curriculum decisions in several ways. They can suggest a new way to look at things that advance a teacher's thinking on curriculum questions. They can help teachers to sort out their personal reactions in a structured way, to understand how their core beliefs lead them to certain conclusions, and to understand why others may disagree with them.

Having a clearer sense of one's own perspective, however, is not enough to enable a teacher to decide what to do in a particular situation. As we have just seen, seemingly conflicting ideas may all have something valuable to contribute to a teacher's understanding. Clearly, a good general education should accomplish many of the aims of all three of the perspectives just described. Even the most extreme advocates of student-centered education would probably agree that students would be harmed by a collapse of the society. They just think that such a collapse is a remote possibility and that education can best forestall such a collapse by nurturing each individual student. But in an extreme situation, such as a war or major social unrest, many who adopt a student-centered position would probably acknowledge the important claims of the society-centered perspective. Similarly, most advocates of society-centered or student-centered views would probably admit, if pressed, that the transmission of knowledge is an important factor in both social and individual welfare. So, there seems to be an underlying compatibility here.

General education is importantly about students, society, and knowledge, and if any one of these components is severely neglected, education is worsened and all components suffer. As circumstances change, one perspective or another requires more emphasis, and those who believe strongly in the primacy of the neglected component will be among the first to speak out and work to correct the problem. The issue seems to be one of priorities and balance among goals and perspectives all of which have something important to contribute.

In addition to perspectives, then, teachers need to develop skill in handling multiple sets of ideas and applying them rigorously and fairly to a variety of practical decisions. Adopting one perspective and applying it consistently is difficult enough, but if teachers must apply several different perspectives and somehow reconcile their conflicting implications, how can that be done? Doing justice to several quite distinct ideas of general education requires a different perspective than does finding the one best idea. It demands a more complex, mature, and sophisticated thought process. Teachers will have to understand several points of view and weigh their sometimes different implications in order to make wise curriculum decisions. Instead of seeking the one true answer, which implies that all others are false, teachers will need to try to make curriculum decisions that seem good from several perspectives and to consider the best tradeoffs of one good for another in their particular circumstances.

One way to view the new kind of reasoning required here is to say that the teacher's goal in thinking about curriculum questions is not to reach a correct general conclusion about curriculum principles, but rather to make fully considered, fair decisions about particular curriculum proposals, as we suggested in chapter 1. This means that the teacher has thought through the decision from several appropriate perspectives, including student-centered, society-centered, and knowledge-centered ones, and sought ways to meet the most important concerns of all interested parties including oneself. When choices must be made among competing aims, the most that any teacher can aspire to do is to state clearly what are the pros and cons of each decision and explain the grounds for choosing one rather than another.

Seeking fully and fairly considered curriculum decisions is not only

harder intellectually, it also demands more of teachers ethically and morally. It demands that teachers develop and practice tolerance of different
perspectives without abandoning their own beliefs and standards. It demands calm and evenhandedness in the midst of controversy. It demands
a willingness to reconsider one's own beliefs and preferences in the course
of debate and in the light of empathy with others' experiences and contrary evidence. It is hard, but it is the best we can ask for in curriculum
matters, and the highest standards are seldom easy to live by.

In the chapters that follow you will have many opportunities to learn
about ideas that have been important in curriculum debates and to practice the skills of applying these ideas to particular hypothetical situations.
Through discussion with others, you should also be able to appreciate
more fully the intellectual and moral demands of striving for the ideal of
fully and fairly considered curriculum decision making yourself.

Before going on, you may want to consider the disputes "Individual
Differences and Equality of Opportunity," "Mass or Class Culture?," and
"National Reports on Education." The case "Go Fly a Kite" provides an
opportunity to explore the idea of curriculum by examining what three
teachers actually do differently with the same class project.

Chapter 4

Conceptualizing Curriculum Phenomena

To this point we have raised two obvious questions: What should be the aims of education and what form should general education take? Now we raise a set of not-so-obvious questions that nevertheless are important for a teacher to think about with regard to curriculum matters. What is knowledge? What sorts of things can be taught and learned? Is a listing of subjects the only or best way to conceptualize a curriculum? What are some useful ways for teachers and curriculum designers to think about the stuff a curriculum is made of? In this chapter we will consider these questions as they illuminate both the instructional and the programmatic aspects of the curriculum.

By *conceptualizing*, we mean developing ways of thinking and talking about something, including making distinctions, defining, naming, and noting significant features. A successful conceptualization is an extremely valuable contribution to the understanding of any phenomenon. For example, while the conceptualization of the phenomena of heat and temperature consisted of the hypothetical weightless fluid phlogiston that was supposed to carry heat and cold from one place to another, progress was slow in many fields of science in which heat played an important part. When these phenomena were conceived differently, in terms of the motion of molecules, research results came more quickly.

In psychology, Freud's conception of the personality as having three fundamental parts—id, ego, and superego—gave us a way to ask certain kinds of questions and to explain certain psychological phenomena we could not have formulated otherwise. His conception also gave us ways to treat certain forms of mental illness. For many purposes ordinary language and common sense provide sufficient means for thinking and talking about curriculum matters. But, as we shall see in this chapter, sometimes more explicit formal conceptualizations of curriculum phenomena are helpful.

One of the best examples of our concern in this chapter, and also one of the most useful answers to the conceptual question of what it is that is taught and learned, was provided at midcentury by the British philosopher Gilbert Ryle in his analysis of the concept of knowledge.[1] Ryle made it clear that there are important differences between knowing *how* to do things and knowing *that* such and such is so. We can learn *that* Columbus discovered America or *that* F = MA fairly directly by being told or reading that these things are so. In school we acquire much information and knowledge of this sort in these direct ways. But we also learn such skills as how to read and how to do scientific experiments, and these require for their mastery many periods of practice over long periods of time in a way that learning facts and formulas does not. Verbal knowledge is useful, but it is not skill knowledge; and sometimes the two are confused by teachers. Verbally learning, and repeating on a test, the steps of the scientific method does not ensure that one can skillfully do experiments; just as getting 100 percent on a test on a book on swimming does not guarantee that the nonswimmer will be able to keep afloat in the water. Learning certain facts about art or literature does not necessarily mean we have learned the requisite skills needed to analyze and appreciate art or literature.

On the other hand, everyone knows of cases in which children are able to mimic the form of a skill without grasping its substance. A teenager offers a glib, formally accurate analysis of the imagery in Shakespeare's *Midsummer Night's Dream* but is only dimly aware of its human significance. A bright elementary school student can design an experiment to answer a scientific question but knows too little science to ask a good question and cannot say which questions have already been answered.

The important point is not that knowing *how* is better or worse than knowing *that*, but that it is important to distinguish between types of knowing and how much of what kind of learning is appropriate for a given situation. The conceptualization of learning as being of these two kinds gives us the capability to distinguish between them and thus enables us to ask and to answer many useful pedagogical questions. There are numerous other applications of this fact-skill conceptualization of curriculum phenomena, but the point here is to see, through this example, what this chapter is about. How we conceive of what is taught and learned is different from how we organize the curriculum and what we aim at, even though these things are all interrelated. Think of the stuff of the curriculum as skills to be learned, as well as facts, and you will see things to do as a teacher that might not have occurred to you otherwise. Think of the most basic (or most difficult) topics you will teach. What approaches are suggested in how to teach these topics when you think of them in light of the *knowing how* and *knowing that* distinction?

Knowledge in Use

In *Democracy and Excellence in American Secondary Education*, Broudy, Smith, and Burnett have provided an interesting way to think about what is learned in school.[2] They were primarily concerned with how the things that are learned in schools are used by the learner in life. They were able to discern four uses of school learning, which they called "replicative," "associative," "applicative," and "interpretive." According to Broudy, Smith, and Burnett, knowledge is used replicatively when we are able, in appropriate situations, to repeat and use what we have learned. We remember that $5 \times 6 = 30$ when needed, just as we "remember" how to read or write or recall the names and sounds of musical instruments when asked to identify them. We can replicate the knowledge and skills we have learned. Much of our knowledge is used this way; much of the teaching in schools is directly aimed at producing the replication of knowledge.

But some things are learned in school indirectly, and students sometimes use things learned in school associatively. We talk to friends about a concert and link together things we learned about composers, instruments, history, and musical forms in ways that they happen to come to mind and not necessarily in the exact way they were taught or learned in school. We also form other kinds of associations in school. Having a mean, strict, or unfeeling teacher of classical music may later lead us to associate discomfort with such music. We also use our learning associatively when we link things previously learned with new things, as we might associate our knowledge of chemical reactions with some news about a new kind of medicine or connect our knowledge of Shakespeare with an episode of a TV sitcom. This is a kind of connecting of bits of knowledge in use and not just a replication.

Knowledge can also be used applicatively, that is, called to mind for use in solving a problem and not just as in answer to a question (replication) or in connection with other things (association). The applicative use of knowledge is aptly demonstrated in the work of the engineer. The engineer uses special knowledge and skills in solving novel problems. Applying knowledge requires seeing the connection between what one knows and what one wants to achieve. It is far easier to replicate and associate knowledge than it is to apply it. Application requires a degree of creativity and flexibility, as well as considerable intelligence. It goes without saying that teaching for knowledge applicability also requires some special qualities. How would you as a teacher try to do it?

Using knowledge interpretively is in one sense applying our knowledge; but it is using knowledge for understanding a situation and not for solving a problem or answering a question. In interpreting, our knowledge is not necessarily applied specifically and directly. It is used as a point of departure, a form of sorting, organizing, and making sense of something. We may have forgotten many of the details of the American Revolution, for instance, but we still may use our general knowledge of that revolt against perceived oppression to understand a rebellion in another country today. We also may use knowledge that we can replicate quite well, like Freud's theories on dreams, say, and use it to interpret a person's dreams. In one sense all of our knowledge is interpretive. It helps us make sense of the world. Perhaps, though, only that knowledge that is meaningful to us can be used interpretively. What do you think? Can you think of examples that would demonstrate using these four conceptions of knowledge in school? In life? Do they overlap and involve each other? Is this a useful conceptualization of curriculum phenomena?

Along these same lines of thinking about how knowledge is used and how this use can demonstrate higher levels of mastery of learning, Benjamin Bloom and his associates have worked out a "Taxonomy of Educational Objectives."[3] Their conceptualization allows teachers and curriculum or measurement specialists to aim at, instruct for, and test different levels of cognitive objectives more systematically. There are some parallels and similarities with the above scheme of uses of knowledge, which we will point out. For our purposes, however, it is more important to see that the conceptualization of curriculum phenomena, in this case the cognitive domain, can become very highly rationalized and our ways of understanding what it is possible to aim at, very fully elaborated.

The taxonomy is arranged in six main levels from lowest to highest. Each higher level is assumed to involve mental processes and uses of knowledge that are more complex and abstract than the ones below it. The first level, simply called "knowledge" and similar to the category of "replication" above, includes objectives that call for recall from memory of such increasingly difficult things as facts, categories, methods, and theories. The second level, "comprehension," requires the student to understand relations and to make sense of the whole. It is akin to the categories of association and interpretation above but different from them, too. Some of the types of mental operations that fall into this category are translation, interpretation, and extrapolation. The typical comprehension objective on a test, for example, requires a paraphrase of a passage or asks questions not directly answered in the passage but inferable from it. It requires a higher level of mental functioning than recall or association.

The third level of the taxonomy is "application" and is similar to Broudy, Smith, and Burnett's similarly named category. It requires students to use some concept or principle by applying it to a new and unfamiliar situation. Since the item to be applied must be remembered, and since the student must understand the new context to which it is being applied, application generally involves the earlier levels of knowledge and comprehension.

The fourth and fifth levels are "analysis" and "synthesis." They cover cognitive tasks and responses in which students must logically break down a complex set of ideas into its constituent elements, relationships, and principles—or build one up from a set of such constituents. The complexes may be arguments, theories, or other such related sets of ideas. An example of the use of analysis would be a history student's untangling and breaking down the causes of the First World War into economic, political, and sociological factors. An example of synthesis would be the student's putting together a set of ideas that expresses a unified position on the causes of war in general.

The sixth and highest level is "evaluation." It consists of objectives that call for qualitative or quantitative judgments about the extent to which given complex entities satisfy appropriate criteria and standards of evidence. In the above history example, evaluation would be used if another student critically examined his classmate's synthesis on the basis of breadth of explanation, plausibility, supporting evidence, cohesion, or other criteria. Judgments, in the taxonomy, are the highest form of mental activity in the cognitive domain.

The taxonomy, along with its companions in the affective and psychomotor domains, can be used to analyze a curriculum to determine whether all the various levels are represented in appropriate proportions. It can also be used in curriculum development, to plan for an appropriate balance; in implementation, to ensure that the balance is being preserved in the classroom and the school; and in evaluation, to develop an appropriate bank of test items.

Conceptualizing the Instructional Process

Looking at knowledge and the use of knowledge as a way of conceptualizing curriculum phenomena can be very helpful in shedding light on ways for thinking about what is taught and what knowledge is. But in a way, it is a consideration of the static elements in curriculum. The dynamics of student interaction with curriculum and instruction over time has also received the attention of theorists and is worth thinking about for teachers. After all, things happen to students over time in their many years of schooling. They move through the curriculum with various beginnings and endings of units and topics, subjects and activities. Education is a temporal and dynamic process. How can we conceptualize that process?

Alfred North Whitehead tried to do just that with his conception of the rhythm of education.[4] Whitehead chastised the schools for teaching students in a way that produced "inert knowledge": knowledge that connected or reacted with nothing in their lives and had little meaning for them. He argued that knowledge had to be meaningfully introduced and thoroughly learned and reflected on by students, rather than collected in encyclopedic fashion. His conception of the rhythm of education can be read as a corrective to such an encyclopedic view of educating and can be applied to the teaching of a subject, of a unit, of a lesson, and even to the elementary, secondary, and postsecondary articulation of education writ large.

"Romance," "precision," "generalization"—these are the terms Whitehead used to characterize the rhythm of education. He believed that one should begin an engagement with any subject in a romantic way, feeling excitement in its presence, being aroused by its attractiveness, and enjoying its company. Thus, for instance, children should be introduced to history or science not by lessons, but by being given exciting stories of past events or fascinating unravelings of nature's ways. The subject then comes alive, is real, and is stimulating to the student and worth the effort of establishing a relationship with over time. Getting to know the subject better and studying it in detail is what the stage of precision is all about. The romantic interest remains and becomes the driving force of self-discipline required for the hard work of studying the subject in detail. As more and more of the parts of the subject are mastered, the stage is set for achieving a perspective on the whole and generalization becomes possible. Some of the same kind of excitement and joy as in the romantic stage is found in the activity of generalization. It is feeling a closeness to the subject because you now know it and understand it so well. Mastery of details allows for comprehension of the whole.

These figurative ways of talking about the educational process and an individual's genuine enjoyment of it will speak to anyone who has ever come really to appreciate and understand some subject, be it history or gardening, science or baseball, literature, cooking, or computing. Whitehead sees the need for the rhythmic cycle of romance, precision, and generalization to repeat itself thoughout the educational process. A lesson or unit (or both) should begin with romantic engagement with the topic, aim at the precision necessary to understand the topic, and result in an understanding of the general relationships within it. One could even view the whole of the formal educational process in these terms. Elementary school is the stage of romance; secondary schooling, precision; and college and university study, generalization.

Whitehead's conceptualization of the educational process speaks neither to what subjects should be taught nor to what knowledge is, but forces a consideration of instruction and curriculum as it affects the student. John Dewey, in his short work *The Child and the Curriculum*, also tried to provide a useful conceptualization of this relationship.[5] He began by pointing to the tensions between traditional and progressive educators: the former stressing the importance of traditional subject matter and the latter making the student's interests and needs more central. Which is more important, the child or the curriculum? Dewey wisely answers, both! The curriculum contains traditional knowledge, but as curriculum, it must be seen as knowledge in relation to the learner and not as something separate from the teaching-learning process. The point of educating is to bring the child into meaningful contact with traditional knowledge while honoring the learner's interests and needs. But how is that to be accomplished?

Dewey used the analogy of an explorer and a map, as we saw earlier, to convey his solution. Recall that, for Dewey, the explorer, like the child, is entering unknown territory. He discovers waterways, mountains, and deserts and is struck with wonder by their majesty and beauty. He suffers hunger and thirst. Strange peoples with strange customs sometimes befriend him and sometimes threaten him. The journey ends, and he produces a map of the territory he has traversed. Deserts, mountains, waterways, and names of tribal territories are all in their proper place. They are lines and words on a two-dimensional surface. The richness of the explorer's experiences is not there.

How often, Dewey wondered, do we give children "maps" void of the experiences that went into the mapmaking? Maps are useful to travelers, of course, but what good is learning the map of a territory you will never travel in? It is the traveling, the experience, that is meaningful and makes knowledge meaningful in its use or its creation. Each child can be like the explorer, creating his or her own meaningful maps of experience in some subject matter area, but according to Dewey, those experiences need to be carefully planned and deftly guided by the teacher, who already knows the territory.

Dewey uses the terms "logical" and "psychological" to conceptualize aspects of subject matter with regard to the teacher and learner. The logical aspect of subject matter is its organization and form—like the map, the product of exploration and inquiry in a field often abstract, containing generalizations and marking relationships. The logical form of subject matter also contains and categorizes specific information about the field. The teacher is trying to lead the student to some grasp of the logical. It is like Whitehead's stage of generalization.

The psychological aspect of subject matter is the learner's experiencing of it. It is like the explorer's journey—seeing and noting things along the way, getting a feeling for the territory, and reaching points where things fall into place and pieces of the map can be drawn. Dewey believed that it is essential for students to have such experiences of the subject matter. He

therefore directs the teacher who is in possession of the logical organization to psychologize it, to provide an environment for the learner that will
call out meaningful experiences of key aspects of the subject matter and
suggest aspects of its logical organization and structure appropriate to the
learner's level of experience. Learning then proceeds from the psychological to the logical, and the child and the curriculum become part of each
other. Before going on, you might want to consider the case "Individualized Learning," in chapter 8.

The Structure of Subjects

In more recent times, Jerome Bruner provided a similar conceptualization
of subject matter, curriculum, and instruction. Bruner believed that "there
is no difference in kind between the man at the frontier [of knowledge]
and the young student at his own frontier, each attempting to understand."[6] In addition, "the foundations of any subject may be taught to
anybody at any age in some form."[7] The key to understanding how this is
possible is Bruner's claim that all subjects have a basic structure, a basic
set of organizing principles, fundamental ideas, and relationships. Mastery of the structure of any field, then, is the key to understanding it, and
Bruner believed that curriculum materials and teaching can be organized
in such a way as to provide students with what they need to discover a
subject's structure on their own. Much like Dewey's explorer and mapma-
ker, anyone at any age can map the major features of an experience of
subject matter, given the proper materials and the teacher's guidance.
"Maps" of structure get richer and more elaborate as students mature and
revisit the field. Bruner used the image of a "spiral curriculum" to suggest
this cyclic returning to a subject and working out of its structure over time
with ever-increasing comprehensiveness. There have been serious questions raised about whether subjects really do have set structures and if
students at all stages of their development really are able to think like the
scholar on the frontier. Nevertheless, Bruner's conceptualization of subject matter as structured is like Whitehead's stage of generalization and
Dewey's logical form of subject matter. Each gives teachers a way to think
about leading students to discover and see the network of basic ideas and
relationships that holds the facts of any subject together.

Meaningful Learning Experiences

To this point, we have implicitly taken a rather traditional view of curriculum phenomena, focusing on the knowledge embodied in the tradition-

al subjects. We have seen curriculum phenomena conceptualized as verbal knowledge, facts and skills, replicative, associative, applicative, interpretive, romantic, precise, generalized, psychologized, discovered, "mapped," and structured. Some progressives have taken a less traditional view of what should be taught and learned.

If we think of what the majority of people need to know to get on in the everyday adult world, it hardly seems to be history or art or physics or chemistry or mastery of any of the traditional subjects. Rather, it seems to be such things as being able to get along with others, perform required tasks at work and at home, stay healthy, solve problems, and enjoy leisure. Moreover, if it is the student's experience that is crucial to determining whether learning takes place in a good way and results in something meaningful, then why not conceive of the stuff of the curriculum not as subjects but as the experiences themselves? This would focus attention, not on the structure of knowledge, but on the structure of qualities of worthwhile learning experiences that would be useful in life. This is precisely what William Heard Kilpatrick tried to do with his elaboration of the project method.

"The Project Method" was an article in the *Teachers College Record*, written by Kilpatrick in 1918 to describe his theory of teaching and curriculum, which embodied the spirit and principles of the early twentieth-century progressive education movement.[8] He characterized the project method as one that combined three elements: wholehearted activity, laws of learning, and ethical conduct with his basic idea that "education *is* life." He sought a way to replace traditional teaching methods, which forced learning, with a method in which learning was achieved without compulsion. In daily life, he argued, we learn from the activities we engage in, from our experiences, not from memorizing or studying, but from doing things with a purpose. He believed that this form of "learning-by-living" and "acting with a purpose" should be brought into the school, thus making school and its curriculum not a preparation for life but an actual part of living and life itself. The means for doing this was the "project method."

To highlight the differences between the project method and traditional teaching methods, Kilpatrick used the example of two boys making a kite, one engaged in a self-initiated, wholehearted, purposeful activity and the other under direct compulsion to produce a replica of a model kite. The physical result of both activities is the same—a kite—but what happens, what is experienced, and what is learned in the process by each differ markedly. The first boy eagerly pursues his single goal, using his own end-in-view, a flyable kite, to guide his decisions and check his work along the way. The finished and flying kite supplies satisfaction and the only standard needed to judge the success of the enterprise. The second boy has, as it were, two purposes: to make a kite and to meet the demands and standards of the teacher. The joy of making a flyable kite often is submerged under the fear of not meeting the teacher's expectations. His kite may fly, but he may be downgraded for not tying the string with the "correct" knot or using too much paste on the paper or some such thing. The first boy takes pride in his school activities, enjoys thinking and working things through, and seeks out new projects to do and to learn from. The second sees school as providing a set of tasks to be performed under compulsion, not for their own sake or value. He dislikes forced working and thinking under the continual stress of possibly being wrong. If he learns something, it is not primarily for himself that he does so, but for others. For Kilpatrick, the curriculum is the experience, not the subject matter.

The role of the teacher, when using the project method, is to guide and help the students through the four phases of their purposeful acts, "purposing, planning, executing, and judging," while avoiding the evils of the older instructional ways and the potential dangers of the new, such as wasting time and choosing projects impossible to complete or lacking in potential for significant learning. By encouraging group projects, such as staging a drama or planting a garden, the teacher can utilize the project method in a social setting, which Kilpatrick believed invariably brings out the need for the group to resolve conflicts, create rules and principles for harmonious action, and respect the rights of others. Such ethical concerns grow out of the situation at hand and are neither sets of rules to be learned by rote nor transgressions to be judged and punished by the teacher. Thus, for Kilpatrick, the project method was a personal, social, moral, and democratic vehicle for learning and for building character—which he took to be the most important of all educational aims.

Program Conceptualization

To this point we have considered various conceptualizations of curriculum phenomena that have lent themselves to illuminating the instructional and methodological side of curriculum thinking. In this concluding section, we will look at a sample of conceptualizations that tend to speak more to the programmatic side. Of course, there is no easily drawn distinction between the two. In one sense, Whitehead's stages lay out a program as well as directing thinking about instruction. Kilpatrick's project method suggests a curriculum program, not of subjects, but of self-initiated and spontaneous group projects. It will be useful, though, to switch perspectives in this section and focus on programmatic conceptions to show the importance of this way of thinking about the curriculum.

How should we think about the curriculum as a programmatic whole? One way, of course, is sequentially and interrelatedly. Certain things seem to be prerequisites for others, and problems of balance and adequacy need to be considered.

One of the most comprehensive conceptualizations of the curriculum ever put forward was Dewey's view of the curriculum as history, geography, and science.[9] At first it might seem that a three-subject curriculum is quite narrow, but we shall see that this is not the case. Dewey was much concerned with the fragmentation of the curriculum into discrete and unconnected subjects. He believed that the curriculum should reflect the interrelatedness of knowledge as it used by human beings to understand and solve problems in the world. There are no solitary math problems in the world, for instance. Only in school is math an isolated set of problems. In the world, there are economic, engineering, and everyday shopping and cooking problems that require math, among other things, for their solution. For Dewey, knowledge is an instrument, not an artifact; it is for use, not for display. To help us see that knowledge is connected to the world, not detached and fragmented, Dewey argued that educators should conceive of the curriculum program along the three comprehensive dimensions of space, time, and order: geography, history, and science.

Human beings exist in space, on the earth, and in the universe. Everything we have come to know about the earth and the space we inhabit is geography for Dewey. This means that subjects such as astronomy and oceanography, as well as physics and chemistry, are connected and aimed at helping us understand nature and solve problems in our human spatial dimension. The temporal dimension represents all of time and human history for Dewey: all we know about ourselves as humans through time, not only by means of our history but also through such subjects as anthropology, sociology, literature, art, psychology, and philosophy. Time and space are the two basic dimensions of the universe and of Dewey's conception of the curriculum.

The world of nature and the world of human culture are other names for these two basic dimensions of our lives. What then of science in Dewey's curriculum? The sciences seem at home in his conceptualization of geography as nature. But science for Dewey is not science in the ordinary sense. It is the highest level of organization that any subject matter can achieve. It is our best collective ordering of knowledge in any subject, in either the spatial or the temporal dimension. The inclusion of this idea of science in Dewey's comprehensive programmatic view of curriculum, then, points to the ideal form and purpose of his curriculum: to put all that is known about everything in its most economical form at the disposal of the learner.

One way of conceptualizing a curriculum program, therefore, is to see it as highly integrated and articulated. Ideas like core curriculum, interdisciplinary studies, and general education programs are related to this approach. Paul Hirst, a British philosopher of education, approaches the integrated curriculum differently from Dewey, arguing that the main business of education is to develop *mind*; mind is our ability to know the world through our shared experiences of the world.[10] Hirst believes that human beings can only experience the world in seven or eight basic ways. In the course of our evolution and history as human beings, he believes, we have developed "forms of knowledge," ways of expressing our knowledge of each of these experiential domains. It is as if we had developed artifactual receptors and processors to sort out and deal with different kinds of experience, much as our natural sense receptors like eyes and ears process the different physical forms, light and sound. Hirst believes that the basic forms of human knowledge are mathematics, physical science, knowledge of persons, literature and fine arts, morals, religion, and philosophy. Each represents our codified ways of experiencing different aspects of the human and natural world we inhabit.

Each has its own network of concepts for capturing some aspect of its realm of experience, and each has ways of properly processing its type of experience as well as having standards for judging claims in its domain. For example, the appreciation of art calls into play a set of concepts, relations, processes, and standards of judgment different from those employed in the appreciation of a logical argument or in the establishment of a scientific claim. The concept of beauty is essential to art, the concept of validity to logic, and the concept of evidence to scientific claims. Different domains of human experience call for different ways to process experience and to justify our claims about that sort of experience. Hirst believes that the curriculum should provide students with an initiation into the various ways of human knowing in each of the forms of knowledge he identifies. His specific rendering of forms of knowledge has been challenged and has changed over the years, but his position has not. The very idea that there are discrete forms of knowledge has also been challenged. Whether he is right or not about discrete forms, he has helped flesh out the idea of what the structure of a subject is. Different subjects do exist and do have their own concepts, theories, methodologies, and standards of judgment.

There are much more limited and concrete ways to come at programmatic conceptualization than those we have considered thus far. Designs of courses, units, and curriculum materials often carry with them specific conceptualizations, even though they are not always overtly identified as such. A reading program based on phonics is different from one based on a whole-word approach in great part because of the way in which the reading phenomena are initially conceptualized. A science program based on discovery learning is different from one based on mastery learning. Conceiving of science as discovery, as a special form of controlled inquiry, is different from conceiving of it as a set of established laws and theories that provide us with the means to predict and control nature if only we can master them.

A limitless set of examples of this kind of programmatic curriculum conceptualization is available in the curriculum materials developed and used in the schools today. Think of some curriculum program or materials you are familiar with and try to identify the programmatic conceptualization that underlies it.

Bruner's *Man: A Course of Study*[11] provides a classic example of programmatic curriculum conceptualization. It is a social studies course designed for upper elementary grades. It does not replicate the traditional social science compartmentalization of studies of man. There is no textbook. There are films, slides, games, stories, and poems that provide students with materials to engage them in thought and inquiry into human nature and human social behavior. Materials on animal behavior provide students with ways to contrast and compare our species with others. A study of life cycle of the salmon, for instance, shows that parental care of the young is not essential to the survival of the species; but some animals, such as herring gulls and baboons, do provide such care, as do humans, and it does seem essential for them. Moreover, a study of baboons shows complex social behavior, not only regarding child rearing but also with respect to providing food, developing interpersonal relationships, territoriality, aggression, and so forth. Learning about and using a distant and distinct culture, the Netsilik Eskimos, as a representative human society, students attempt to discern those aspects of human nature and social behavior that seem universal from those that seem to arise because of environment and culture. The whole course is directed toward allowing students to discover how humans are distinctive from and what we share with other living creatures. This conceptualization of social studies suggests and justifies a very different curriculum from the traditional one.

Perhaps the most radical conceptualization of the curriculum from a programmatic point of view was Kilpatrick's, and it provides a fitting way to end this chapter by challenging your thinking. As we have seen in our discussion of the project method, Kilpatrick saw purposeful life experiences to be the essential stuff of the curriculum. But he believed that purposes had to come genuinely from the students themselves and should not be artificially provided by teachers. Therefore, Kilpatrick reasoned, there should be no preset curriculum. The curriculum should be created on the spot, out of the needs and purposes of the students![12] What do you think? Would such a curriculum be consistent with the other important educational aims for which schools have traditionally assumed a responsibility? Would the means chosen by Kilpatrick to achieve the end of a meaningful education be the only way of achieving this aim? If not, would it be the best way? A good way? What factors should enter into an educator's decision to adopt Kilpatrick's proposal? Before going on you might want to consider the case "Grading Policies" or the dispute "A Social Studies Curriculum," in chapter 8.

Chapter 5

Procedures for
Curriculum Making

In this chapter our focus shifts again. This time it is a shift from *what* and *why* to *how*, from a search for answers to the primary curriculum questions of what to teach and why, to a search for useful *methods* for finding the answers. If you are not certain what the curriculum for a school or for a subject should be, or if people of good will disagree about it, how might you proceed? Are there different ways of figuring out what the curriculum should be? If so, are some of these ways better than others? How should you go about making a curriculum? Where should you start and what should you do?

Sources of Curriculum Making

Given the task of making your own curriculum as a teacher, you might decide to spin the curriculum out of your head, like a spider using its inner resources to produce an intricately patterned web. After all, you know your subject matter and you have ideas about what students at the age level you will teach should learn. Or you might, like an ant, go about gathering bits and pieces of curriculum materials relevant to your subject and grade level and pile them up for use as you need them. Once they are collected, you might even organize them in a way that seems appropriate. Of course, you could just go directly to the curriculum guide provided by your school or district. Not a bad idea sometimes, but how did its makers proceed when they designed it? Like the spider? Like the ant? In some other way? This is our concern in this chapter.

Curriculum making can be subject-, learner-, or society-centered. We have seen some examples of these general orientations toward curriculum making in previous chapters. The Committee of Ten, for instance, approached the task of curriculum making from a *subject-centered* point of view. Once the aim of college preparation was posited and a set of relevant academic subjects determined, the real work of curriculum making began. Experts were recruited to break down their subjects into units that then were arranged sequentially by appropriate grade level. In the history curriculum, for example, the Committee of Ten prescribed for the fifth and sixth grades an introduction to history through biography and mythology; seventh grade, American history; eighth grade, Greek and Roman history; ninth grade, medieval and modern French history; tenth grade, medieval and modern English history; eleventh grade, American history; twelfth grade, civics.[1] These in turn were internally broken down into prescribed subunits.

The progressive educators' emphasis on the child brought with it a different approach to curriculum construction. Given the perceived need for the learner to be fully and genuinely engaged in learning by experience, progressives sought out activities, materials, and projects that would provide the proper environment for this to happen. Laboratory and experimental schools became places where the traditional subject-centered curriculum was set aside and experiential, *learner-centered* approaches and materials were created and tried out. Unlike the armchair procedures of curriculum making used by subject-matter specialists, the progressives believed in hands-on curriculum making carried out in actual school and classroom situations. Unfortunately, their work was more trial and error than scientifically controlled experiment.

During the early part of this century, however, there was a sustained attempt to make curriculum construction more rigorously scientific. Part of that effort was *society-centered*, to the extent that it looked to the norms and practices of society to determine what the curriculum should be. For instance, surveys were made of curricula in many schools, allowing a district to compare itself with other schools and see if it was up to date and at the norm. Also, scientific studies of such things as the most commonly used words and the arithmetic skills most used by adults in everyday life provided hard data for textbook writers and curriculum developers to design graded work in reading, spelling, and math. Of course, there were other society-centered approaches, more "aims oriented," which differed from the data-based scientific approach. Many educational philosophers looked to what they hoped society would be—democratic, moral, self-sufficient, unified, peopled with productive happy citizens—and proposed curricula designed to achieve such ends. The work of Plato, Dewey, and Bantock and that of the Harvard Committee, for example, used this approach. But the scientific approach was and still is a very influential approach to curriculum making.

A classic example of the "scientific" approach to curriculum making was Franklin Bobbitt's 1924 book, *How to Make a Curriculum*.[2] To determine the curriculum, he used time-and-motion-study techniques, drawn from "scientific management" practices of that period, to study the best performances of well-educated people. This was how occupations were studied; why not study the educated in the same way? If bricklaying was under study, for example, the bricklayer with the greatest output of high-quality work would be identified on the basis of records and observation of performance. He would then be studied in minute detail to discover how he accomplished his feats, and other workers would be trained to follow his method. It seemed to many educators at the time to be a very realistic and useful way to find what was needed to make a curriculum that would produce educated people who acted wisely and effectively in the world. The performance-based and competency-based teacher education movement of the 1970s repeated this mode of curriculum construction.

The Tyler Rationale

By far the most influential set of ideas about how to make a curriculum is embodied in the "Tyler rationale." In fact, Daniel Tanner and Laurel Tanner[3] claim that the Tyler rationale is *the* paradigm, *the* dominant model of twentieth-century thought about curriculum design. A paradigm is a set of guiding ideas that are generally accepted at a given time by those who work in a field. Until a better model is developed and accepted, a paradigm remains dominant, even though other models may exist at the same time and have some marginal support. The concept of a paradigm often carries with it the idea that it is difficult, if not impossible, for those in a given field to think about their subject in non-paradigm-structured ways. Since Tanner and Tanner claim that the Tyler rationale (including variations on its basic formula) is *the* accepted way of handling curriculum development in our day, it may be difficult to think about curriculum making any other way. Although criticisms have been offered of the Tyler rationale and competing models offered, none, in our judgment, have seriously challenged its dominance. As we describe the Tyler rationale, ask yourself if you can think of a different way to describe sensible procedures for curriculum making that is not just a variation on Tyler's scheme. If you cannot, you will see how deeply ingrained this way of thinking about curriculum making has become.

In 1949, Ralph Tyler published the syllabus for his course Education 260—Basic Principles of Curriculum and Instruction, which he gave at the University of Chicago. Tyler refers to this monograph as a "rationale." He claimed that "it is not a manual for curriculum construction since it does not describe and outline in detail the steps to be taken by a given school or college that seeks to build a curriculum," but, rather, is a way of "viewing, analyzing, and interpreting" the program of an educational institution.[4]

Although Tyler denies that his rationale is a method to be followed step-by-step, it has been so interpreted and so followed by many.

Tyler organizes his rationale around four fundamental questions, which he claims must be answered in developing any curriculum:

1. What educational purposes should the school seek to attain?
2. What educational experiences can be provided that are likely to attain these purposes?
3. How can these educational experiences be effectively organized?
4. How can we determine whether these purposes are being attained?[5]

In other words, Tyler is making it clear that when constructing a curriculum you need first to think about your aims and objectives (1) and second about the kind of subject matter or experiences that will most likely help students achieve those objectives (2). These then need to be put together programmatically (3), and, finally, the results of using your curriculum need to be evaluated in some way (4).

In describing these procedures for curriculum making, Tyler does not himself suggest what purposes the school should seek to attain. Rather, he suggests that each school should determine its own purposes. He recommends that those involved in the determination of purposes seek guidance from studies of the student as a learner, from studies of contemporary life outside the school, and from specialists in the various subjects. (These are the same three sources we described in some detail above.) Then, suggestions derived from all these avenues of inquiry should be screened and reduced to a small number of "consistent, highly important objectives." Tyler also proposes that a school develop a statement of educational philosophy and that the school's philosophy be used as a set of standards to "screen" the objectives derived from this first step in the process. This will ensure that each objective is in harmony with the school's general philosophy and ideal aims.

He suggests that what is known about the psychology of learning provides another "screen," enabling us to determine what actually can be learned and what cannot, which goals are practicable for schools and which take too long or cannot be attained by students at that age level, and so on. Since learning theories sometimes differ among themselves, a school may need to select its psychology of learning to harmonize with its philosophy. For instance, a humanistically oriented school would probably find behaviorist psychology to be a philosophically unacceptable approach to learning. Having a consistent as well as a comprehensive view is important.

When objectives have been determined, Tyler recommends that they be stated in such a way that they specify precisely and unambiguously just what is supposed to be learned. This will enhance the possibility of accurate assessment later on. He also recommends that objectives should specify the changes to be brought about in the student clearly enough to provide a way to judge through evaluation whether the student has really attained these objectives.

Once objectives are developed, it becomes possible to determine what learning experiences might lead to their attainment. Tyler suggests that this process is a creative one in which the teacher "begins to form in his mind a series of possibilities of things that might be done."[6] These are written down, elaborated, and then checked against the objectives to see whether they give students the opportunity to acquire the behavior stated in the objectives. They can also be checked to determine if they are likely to lead to the effect for which they are intended. And they should be screened for economy. Those experiences that meet these tests are ready for the next step—organization.

If learning experiences are to produce a cumulative impact on students, they must be organized so that experiences in one class or subject are in harmony with experiences in others and so that experiences from month to month and from year to year result in steady growth. Important objectives need to be addressed time and time again in different ways, so that they are learned thoroughly (the principle of continuity). Successive learning experiences should build on one another, taking students more deeply into the subject each time (the principle of sequence). And the various learning experiences the student encounters in school ought to be coherently and constructively related to one another (the principle of integration). An education is more than a collection of unrelated skills and knowledge.

Tyler recommends that curriculum developers select a type of organizing element appropriate to their task and then use each element to build continuity, sequence, and integration into the curriculum. For example, he suggests that concepts and skills have been important types of organizing elements in mathematics. Social studies curricula often include values, as well as concepts and skills, among their organizing elements. On a larger scale, the entire school program needs an organizing structure. In secondary schools the organizing structure is usually subject matter fitted into a daily schedule of courses. In elementary schools the organizing structure is often more flexible, sometimes nongraded, usually under the immediate direction of a teacher or team who are free to schedule the days and weeks of the year as they see fit within broad limits. Tyler believes that each school should decide upon an organizing structure that suits it. Thus Tyler's rationale tries to remain value free even as it prescribes in detail how to develop a curriculum.

Evaluation, the last concern in the Tyler rationale, is a process for determining whether the curriculum is achieving the desired results.

Through evaluation, the assumptions and hypotheses on which the program has been built are checked, as well as the efficacy of the particular means chosen to put the program into effect. Evaluation involves an appraisal of the student's actual behavior. Furthermore, it requires an appraisal at several different times to secure evidence of the permanence of the learning achieved. A variety of methods may be used—tests, work samples, questionnaires, records, and so forth. Evaluation instruments should be tailored to the school's objectives. The instruments should be objective, in the sense that different individuals administering a given instrument to the same students should receive the same results. Results of evaluation should be used to indicate strengths and weaknesses in the school program and to plan for revision.

Having provided this fuller description of the Tyler rationale, we can now summarize its elements and emphasize its key features: state *objectives*, *select* learning activities, *organize* learning activities, and develop means of *evaluation*. It should be clear that even though Tyler takes into account all that we have considered thus far and more (evaluation), his is a different way of thinking about the curriculum. He makes no commitment to certain ideal aims, specific objectives, a particular program, or one conceptualization of curriculum phenomena over another, as other theorists that we have considered thus far have done. His commitment is to a highly rationalized, comprehensive *method* for arriving at logical and justifiable curricula of many different kinds. In this way, the Tyler rationale reflects the dominant scientific mode of thinking in the twentieth century, which claims objectivity and impartiality and separates itself from value determination.

In these ways Tyler's rationale concentrates on the *how* of curriculum making, not the *what* of the curriculum itself. Tyler assumes that curricula will vary from one school to another and, indeed, that they should vary. The curriculum that is good for a school in rural Illinois may not be good for a school in New York City. What can be and should be similar, however, are rigorous and thorough methods to arrive at the different curricula. According to Tyler, each school should use its own philosophy and values, as well as the facts of its particular situation, to determine its curriculum. Do you agree? You might want to consider the dispute "To Each His Own," in chapter 8, as well as the case "The Geometry Curriculum."

There have been numerous variations on the methodological theme of the Tyler rationale, which helps support Tanner and Tanner's claim that it has become the dominant paradigm for curriculum development in the twentieth century. In *The Teacher–Empiricist*, for instance, James Popham emphasizes evaluation and stresses the need for teachers to develop clear and precise behavioral objectives that are measurable and puts the Tyler rationale to work in describing effective teaching.[7] In a value-free, neutral vein similar to Tyler, Popham describes the procedures a teacher should use to make his or her own curricular and instructional decisions. Popham suggests that objectives be derived from Bloom's taxonomy, or from going through the first step of the Tyler rationale, or from a bank of behavioral objectives like the one he himself and his colleagues created at UCLA, called the "Instructional Objectives Exchange."[8] Next, the students are pretested to see where they are in relation to the objectives chosen. Then instructional decisions regarding means for reaching the objectives are made and executed. Finally, evaluation of measurable changes in student behaviors are made. Thus, while specifically using the Tyler rationale within it, Popham's theoretical description of how to teach effectively is almost a mirror reflection of the Tyler rationale in general. Objectives, selection, organization, and evaluation procedures are prescribed. Tanner and Tanner's claim that the Tyler rationale is *the* paradigm of curriculum development is a compelling one. Can you think of an effective way to describe teaching or curriculum development without treating objectives, selection, organization, and evaluation?

Schwab's Practical and Eclectic Approach

Even Schwab—who argues that curriculum theorists have taken the field astray by seeking general theories of curriculum development rather than answers to specific, everyday curriculum problems—admits that his ideas, which sound radical, are quite compatible with and "immanent" in the Tyler rationale.[9] Schwab states flatly that the curriculum field is "unable, by its present methods and principles, to continue its work and contribute significantly to the advancement of education. . . . [It] has reached this unhappy state by inveterate, unexamined, and mistaken reliance on *theory*."[10] The field will only recover its ability to contribute to the improvement of American education "if curriculum energies are in large part diverted from theoretic pursuits . . . to three other modes of operation . . . which differ radically from the theoretic, . . . the *practical*, the *quasi-practical*, and the *eclectic*.[11]

It is difficult to do justice briefly to Schwab's proposed three interrelated alternatives, but essentially they amount to careful consideration of a variety of alternative courses of action in *specific situations*. Actions to be taken in these situations should be determined in light of specific factual knowledge about the situation as well as whatever we can find, regardless of the source, for understanding and interpreting both the actions and the situation. Merits of competing theories are to be weighed for their applicability and usefulness in this particular case. This is all to be accomplished through deliberation, much as a jury deliberates upon a verdict once the evidence is in.

Instead of seeking a curriculum theory consisting of a rationalized set of universal principles, Schwab urges us to be practical and seek good decisions and actions in particular cases of curriculum policy or practice. We should not expect to find any sweeping, general resolution to abstract classes of curriculum problems, any more than we would expect to find such complete answers to questions of what candidate to elect, whom to marry, or what job to take. Our choices in such matters shape our lives, they call for our best intellectual efforts; but they do not call for the application of any political theory, theory of spouse-selection, or theory of job choice. Likewise, Schwab argues, curriculum decisions do not require a curriculum theory.

In studying how curriculum development groups actually worked, Walker found that they did not follow Tyler's four steps.[12] In fact, many curriculum groups *never* stated objectives at all; and those that did generally did so near the end of their work, as a way of expressing their purpose to teachers, rather than at the beginning, as the fundamental starting point of their work. Their starting point appeared to be a set of beliefs and images they shared—beliefs about the content; about the students, their needs, and how they learn; about schools, classrooms, and teaching; about the society and its needs; and images of good teaching, of good examples of content and method, and of good procedures to follow. They spent a great deal of time stating and refining these beliefs, which comprised what Walker called their "platform."

Their work consisted of proposing courses of action they might take in curriculum development and discussing the pros and cons of each proposal. Naturally, their discussions drew heavily on their platform. In this way their deliberations were relative to a particular set of beliefs and images not subject to debate—just as a jury's deliberations are relative to the law, which they must accept as given. They also tried to reach judgments about the best courses of action the same way a jury tries to reach a judgment of guilt or innocence—by weighing all the facts. In short, they used deliberation, just as Schwab had suggested they should.

Schwab's deliberative process of curriculum planning may be different from, but is not necessarily inconsistent with, Tyler's rationale. It could be seen as one way of determining objectives, for example. But it brings to the foreground aspects of the process that are consigned to a minor place in Tyler's model—deliberation, judgment, focus on the particulars of the situation, the need for considering a variety of concepts and ideas. Schwab regards both means and ends as mutually determining one another, whereas Tyler insists that our actions (means) must be adjusted to our objectives (ends). Tyler's model requires us to make our objectives public and explicit from the start, so that we and everyone else can see whether we have succeeded or not in our attempts to realize them. In Schwab's deliberative process, however, it is possible, indeed likely, that stating objectives will be slighted and done as an afterthought, if at all.

While Schwab's view of curriculum making is less linear and comprehensive and more flexible and dialectical than the Tyler rationale, the same kinds of questions that Tyler asks need to be addressed at some point in deliberation. We still need to ask what our purposes are and how we might achieve them; we still need to find out if we have done so in our particular setting. Schwab himself recognizes this, and so the dominance of the Tyler rationale in thinking about curriculum making seems to be unshaken.

Freire's Emancipation Approach

However, more radical proposals, quite different from the Tyler rationale, have been made for curriculum construction procedures. For example, Paulo Freire is a Brazilian educator who developed a method for teaching illiterate adult peasants in the backward northeastern region of Brazil. He was exiled for his work in 1964. His book *Pedagogy of the Oppressed*[13] presents his political and philosophical ideas as well as the pedagogical practices he has developed. Here we shall be concerned mainly with the method he describes for developing a curriculum whose main purpose is to stimulate and sustain *critical consciousness* in people. It will be necessary to explain briefly what he means by this concept.

Freire's fundamental concern is with the liberation of poor, powerless, and ignorant people who have been subject to slavelike domination by wealthy people. He believes that an oppressive view of social reality is imposed by the dominant groups on the oppressed, making it impossible for them to perceive and assess their situation or even to think it can be otherwise. This version of social reality is inculcated through words, images, customs, myths, popular culture, and in countless obvious and subtle ways that pervade public life. The oppressed accept this version as reality and are psychologically devastated by it. By accepting the dominant view, they come to think of themselves as worthless, helpless, and inferior. They acquire the personality traits characteristic of oppressed people: fatalism, self-deprecation, and emotional dependence.

The primary task of education, for Freire, is to overcome these attitudes and replace them with traits of active freedom and human responsibility. This cannot be done by treating the oppressed as objects whose behaviors are to be transformed by the educators. Rather, they must be treated as active human agents who deserve our help, so that they can achieve their own liberation. They need to be awakened "to see themselves as men engaged in the ontological and historical vocation of becoming more fully human."[14] This is to be accomplished through dialogue. The task of the educator is problem posing—"posing of the problems of men in their relations with the world."[15] The "students" and their "teachers" must become collaborators, co-investigators developing together their consciousness of reality and their images of a possible, better reality. This ability to step back from an unconscious acceptance of things as they are and to perceive the world critically, even in the midst of pervasive, powerful, subtle forces tending to distort and oppress, is what Freire means by attaining *critical consciousness*.

How, then, to develop a curriculum to foster this critical consciousness in the masses? Freire proposes that a team of educators work with the people of a given locality to develop *generative themes* that reflect their view of reality, based on and taken from the local way of life. First, the team members meet with representatives of the people to be educated to discuss their plans and to secure their permission and cooperation. Members of the team visit the locality and observe how the people live—at home, at work, at church, at play; the language used; people's actual behavior; their postures, dress, relationships. Observers look for anything and everything that indicates how the people construe reality and their situations, so that they later can help them raise their consciousness about such things.

Preliminary findings of these local investigations are presented in a series of evaluation meetings held in the locality, involving members of the team and volunteers from the community. As the observers report the incidents they observed and their feelings and perceptions about them, the group discusses various ways these incidents might be interpreted, ways they might reveal other aspects of the people's lives. From these discussions emerge the contradictions that, if clearly perceived, would reveal to the people their oppressed state. These, then, become the initial themes to be used in discussion and in literacy training.

The investigators, having identified the themes and collected specific materials from the local community related to them, then return to the community to present them to the people to be educated in a series of "thematic investigation circles." In these meetings, the people discuss the concrete materials presented to them. The coordinator of the team elicits views and challenges speakers to reflect on the relationship of their views to those of others. Freire uses the example of alcoholism. Instead of railing against drinking, participants are encouraged to express their views about a specific incident. In the course of the discussion, comments are made that reveal dimly perceived relationships with other matters. Comments like "He's got to do something to blow off steam" lead to acknowledgment of stresses centered around work—no job security, low wages, feelings of exploitation—reasons for the need to "blow off steam."

The work of the thematic investigation circles having been completed, an interdisciplinary team of psychologists, sociologists, educators, and nonprofessional volunteers identifies the generative themes to be used as the curriculum in the actual instruction and develops curriculum materials—readings, tapes, visuals—related to each theme that can be used by the teachers who will work in the next phase, "culture circles."

These concrete materials are then presented to the culture circles as a focus for discussion. Sometimes they are dramatized. Always they are presented as problems, not as answers. Thus the people's own lives are reflected back to them, but this time in a way that encourages critical awareness of their situation, not passive acceptance of an oppressive interpretation. Their consciousness is raised, and they are encouraged to question their world.

For the emancipation theorists, the aim of education is raising the critical consciousness of the oppressed so they can free themselves from a life of domination by others. They believe that this is the proper aim for the education not only of the peasants of Brazil, but also for the poor and the oppressed in large cities, for migrant workers, for factory workers in all parts of the world, and for all anywhere who have learned not to question their lot in life.

It should be clear that Freire's curriculum ideas are not purely procedural. Unlike Tyler, Freire espouses a definite educational aim—consciousness raising. He would not be content to let users of his model select whatever goals they wished. But, like Tyler's, his model does not specify the curriculum in advance, and it does provide a set of procedures for determining specific curriculum goals and content. So, Freire's plan for curriculum making is a combination of the procedural and the rationalizing approaches to curriculum determination. Yet Freire's procedures seem quite different from Tyler's. But are they really? Would not someone following Freire's procedures also eventually select some goals, choose methods for teaching, organize, and evaluate? Is this radical approach to curriculum construction a variation on the Tyler rationale, or is it a truly different way to think about how to make a curriculum? If you were working in an inner-city school or a rural school with many children of migrant workers, would a consciousness-raising curriculum be compatible with a more traditional curriculum centered on subject matter? Would you follow Tyler's procedures or Freire's? Are they basically similar or are they fundamentally different?

The Politics of Curriculum Making

Thus far in this chapter we have looked at procedures for curriculum making from the point of view of the curriculum user. We might call it an instrumental or technical view of prescribing procedures for the curriculum maker. Curriculum making is also a public and political process, however, and curriculum thinkers have tried to describe the political dimension of curriculum making as it might work in a pluralistic, decentralized, democratic society like the United States. Ending this chapter with a look at curriculum making from this broader and more descriptive point of view will help us turn to another way of thinking about curriculum that we will treat in the next chapter.

John Goodlad and Maurice Richter exemplify a broader descriptive approach to thinking about procedures for curriculum making that they put to use in politically prescriptive ways. They believe that curriculum decision making should be assigned explicitly to the proper level and office of the legitimate decision-making bodies.[16] They distinguish three levels of curriculum decision making: the instructional, the institutional, and the societal. The instructional level consists of decisions made by teachers, students, and others who experience the instruction at first hand. This has been our focus in this chapter thus far. At one step removed from the instructional level, however, we will find those decisions that affect the institutions within which instruction takes place: the school, the school district, the office of education for a county or a state. Institutional-level decisions may affect classrooms in powerful ways, but decisions made at this level are necessarily made in ignorance of the specifics of any learning environment. The local board of education plays the pivotal role in institutional-level decision making in the United States, mediating between larger societal influences and the instructional level of decision and action.

Finally, we come to the societal level of curriculum decision making. Here decisions are made whose consequences pervade the other levels, but that are necessarily still further removed from the specifics of teaching and learning. This level includes decisions, made by various controlling agencies and sanctioning bodies, about the form of educational institutions, certification, national testing for college entrance, funding for curriculum development, and so on. The procedures for curriculum decision making as described by Goodlad and Richter form a complex series of transactions among these different levels. The curriculum as it is enacted in the classroom must be seen as the result of many decisions made at each of these various levels.

In their discussion of how decisions about aims, learning experiences, curriculum, organization, and evaluations should be made—at what levels, using what data—Goodlad and Richter describe a process that they claim is basically an extension of Tyler's rationale across a broader range of curriculum-determining entities. They show us that curriculum making is a complex political and social process as well as an intellectual and educational one. But is it not strange that even they see a close relationship between their ideas and Tyler's! Before going on you might want to consider the cases "Do Procedures Make a Difference?" and "Teaching 'Relevant' Literature," in chapter 8. You might also try to answer the thematic question of this chapter about the pervasiveness of the Tyler rationale in our thoughts about procedures for curriculum making.

Chapter 6

Explaining and Critiquing Curriculum Practices

The type of thinking about curriculum that we turn to in this chapter is frankly academic and scholarly in orientation. However, it is also found in the popular press, in politics, and in teachers' conversations in school staff rooms. When we wonder how things got the way they did in schools, "why Johnny can't read," or if our children are "growing up absurd," we are at the same time seeking explanations for the current state of educational affairs and being critical of them. We want to know what happened, why it happened, and if something can be done to improve matters. Developing a critical attitude toward curriculum practices is an important thing for an educator to do. We believe that it is the only responsible and ethical position for people who are engaged as professionals in the human services of education to adopt. So, in this chapter, we will introduce you to some of the major forms of contemporary curriculum research, scholarship, and criticism. We believe that the work of scholars of education can help you to examine your practices critically and to consider reflectively the criticisms offered by others. Scholarly explanations of education can also provide you with deeper understanding of the important work you will engage in as a teacher.

Every ten years or so in our recent history, the American educational system seems to receive intense public scrutiny in the form of national reports on education. Various commentators, commissions, study groups, foundations, prominent authors, educators, and reporters try to find out what is wrong with our educational system and explain how to set it right. These recurring "crises" and the critiques they generate sometimes have a great impact on curriculum practice. The new math and the updated science curricula of the 1960s were ushered in on a wave of public concern created by the launching of the first satellite by the Soviet Union in 1957. Head Start, bilingual education, and other compensatory education programs resulted from the ferment associated with the civil rights struggle in the late 1960s and early 1970s. Various proposals for testing students and teachers were instituted as part of the accountability movement in the 1970s. In the 1980s we saw, once more, widespread public concern about the quality of our schools and more proposals, such as those contained in *A Nation at Risk* and Boyer's *High School*, that called for the raising of standards.[1]

Meanwhile, scholars and researchers in education carry on continual studies of the curriculum that the general public seldom hears about but that often influence the authors of the next round of popular proposals. This is a literature by and for professional educators that speaks to our need to understand and be critical of our own practices. Our goal in this chapter is to introduce you to some examples of this literature, so that you can begin to appreciate its potential to inform your own professional judgment in curriculum matters.

A Critique of the Tyler Rationale

Criticism, both in the narrow sense of finding fault and in the wider sense of analyzing and evaluating, is an important form of curriculum theorizing carried out by curriculum specialists. Instead of proposing a curriculum and rationalizing it, the scholarly critic assesses the strong and weak points of either an existing curriculum theory or an existing program. Sometimes recommendations for improving either the theory or the program emerge from such criticism, making it a kind of amendment to the original, if the changes proposed are minor, or a substitute proposal otherwise. But even when scholarly critics only point out inadequacies, they do us a service by suggesting problems with a theory or program that need our attention. We should not depend on a theory or continue mindlessly to follow a curriculum program if either has serious flaws.

Herbert Kliebard's critique of the Tyler rationale offers a good illustration of the form that curriculum criticism by an informed and thoughtful scholar takes.[2] Kliebard criticizes Tyler's use of the concept of needs to justify the selection of objectives. He argues that appeals to students' needs are a way of seeming to provide a factual basis for what is essentially a value judgment. To claim that a survey of student reading habits that reveals a high proportion of comic-book readers shows a "need" for developing broader and deeper reading interests is, in Kliebard's analysis, simply a way of cloaking a value judgment about "inferior" reading matter in a mantle of scientific objectivity. Kliebard considers as another sleight of hand Tyler's notion that a philosophy of education can be used as an *objective* screen for choosing the worthiest among many possible objectives. In fact, Kliebard argues, such a choice is simply another way of saying that one must ultimately choose in light of one's own values, not by some objective yardstick. In these ways, Kliebard forces us to reflect on Tyler's claims about value neutrality and objectivity.

Kliebard also challenges Tyler's assumption that learning experiences can be "selected and organized." Experiences are the unique and not wholly predictable result of interactions among students, teachers, and their environment. How can they, then, be selected or organized? Activities, tasks, and assignments perhaps can be selected and organized, but not experiences. Thinking they can may mislead us as curriculum developers and as teachers.

Kliebard also questions the wisdom of an evaluation that merely checks on the attainment of previously stated objectives. He quotes John Dewey's claim that achieving the aim of an action is not necessarily the most important of its consequences; ancillary or concomitant results are often more important. For example, learning the names of musical instruments and classical forms of music (a unit's objectives) may not be as important as a student's learning or not learning to appreciate music, as a result of exposure to such instruction about music.

Scholarly criticism as a form of curriculum thinking commonly draws upon a variety of sources and uses methods drawn from the humanities—primarily philosophy, history, and literary criticism. In his criticism of Tyler, for example, Kliebard draws upon such sources. In some cases, as in his criticism of Tyler's use of the concept of "needs," he relies on a close analysis of the text itself, much in the manner of classical scholars or analytic philosophers. In other cases, he invokes the authority of other educational theorists, as with his reference to Dewey in the matter of concomitant outcomes. He also uses historical studies as a basis for criticism. For instance, Kliebard claims that Tyler makes an error when he says that the Committee of Ten Report recommended a program for the college-bound. He points out that the Committee specifically stated that it was proposing one program for all secondary school students, regardless of their future careers, and that this is sufficient evidence to prove that they were not designing a college preparatory curriculum—even though some critics labeled it elitist and charged it with being suitable only for the college-bound.

Criticism normally also offers a summary assessment of what it has been critical about: All things considered, what should we make of it or do about it? Performing this critic's function, Kliebard suggests that Tyler's rationale has continued to influence educators in spite of its serious flaws because Tyler's ideas "skirt the pitfalls to which the doctrinaire are subject" and strikes appealing "compromises between warring extremes." Kliebard assesses the Tyler rationale as "an eminently reasonable framework for developing a curriculum," but he argues that it should not be "*the* universal model of curriculum development." A new model, a new paradigm, Kliebard feels, is "long overdue."[3]

Do you agree with Kliebard's criticisms of Tyler? Do you feel the same way about Tyler's rationale as you did before you read about Kliebard's critique? Do you see the value of scholarly critique?

Curriculum and Criticism of Modern Life

We have seen that one function of scholarship is to criticize accepted views. Nothing should be considered immune from honest critique. In fact, tenure for academics and teachers has frequently been justified primarily on the grounds that it is important to protect them against dismissal for being critical and espousing or teaching unpopular views. The role of scholar as gadfly is as old as Socrates and as honored as any academic tradition. Our next example of curriculum scholarship does more than criticize another theory, however; it criticizes the very society that sustains the institution of schooling.

Michael Apple, in *Ideology and Curriculum*, claims that the primary function of schools is really "cultural reproduction," that is, reproducing in each new generation the social patterns and power relations of the prior one.[4] For Apple, the dominant fact of our current social order is the central role that capital, wealth, and economic power play in it. The United States, he maintains, is governed by the interests of capital, of big business and corporations. They control the media, production, consumption, and the distribution of goods. These dominant interests exercise *hegemony*, literally "rule" or "authority," and exert a predominant influence on all individuals in the society through sometimes subtle but always powerful mechanisms of domination in which, Apple believes, the schools play a major part.

Schooling functions, he maintains, to reproduce and sustain an unjust, inequitable, and inhumane maldistribution of power. It helps those in power to maintain their power and trains those without power to accept their underclass station in life. It does this, in part, by teaching a selective version of knowledge. A partial and biased set of facts is purveyed as the complete, neutral, objective truth. For example, history is taught so as to glorify those who agree with our leaders and vilify those who do not. Science is taught in a way that produces useful workers for a technological economy. Also, the structure of school as an institution acts subtly to control those in it. Teachers and students are kept busy with details, enmeshed in bureaucratic rules, and required to follow the dictates of plans and materials imposed from the outside until they become accustomed to doing what the authorities expect of them. Students who question or challenge their role and status within the school are subjected to disciplinary action. Teachers who do so are reprimanded or given poor evaluations. Everyone learns to be part of the system and to assume one's "proper" role in relation to authority without learning about the underlying mechanisms that structure our social relations.

Apple argues that knowledge is a form of cultural capital. Schools legitimize certain kinds of knowledge by including them in the formal curriculum. By defining the knowledge everyone is expected to have, schools confer special status on that knowledge which is important to the dominant interests, while neglecting and denying this status to knowledge that may be equally or more important to other segments of the society. Thus, schools place higher value on science and vocational subjects than on the arts or crafts. In teaching history and social studies, harmony and consensus are emphasized and conflict minimized, leaving students with the impression of a society in which people are content, happy, and in agreement on most things. According to Apple, school thus plays a pivotal role in preserving the cultural capital of the dominant economic forces of the society.

Schools also help to preserve the existing power relations of society through a hidden curriculum. In analyzing children's first school experiences in kindergarten, Apple notes that "the four most important skills that the [kindergarten] teacher expected the children to learn during those opening weeks were to share, to listen, to put things away, and to follow the classroom routine."[5] These are all efforts to socialize children, to control them, not to teach them anything substantive. He notes that children had no part in organizing the classroom activity and were unable to affect these activities. While attractive materials were present, the teacher's structuring of time and activities effectively made them unavailable. Within weeks, children in this kindergarten class distinguished between work and play within the classroom. Play was freely chosen activity. Work was something you were told to do and had to do, where you were supervised and your performance evaluated. What could more directly prepare children for a life as workers in an industrial society?

Apple's analysis and critique spring from his commitment to a set of moral and political ideals. For Apple, scholarship is a tool for exposing and thus undermining deceptive but accepted "truths." He argues that educational research and scholarship should not be neutral but should take an advocacy position on such issues as students' rights, teachers' rights, and the rights of oppressed minorities. He urges those who work on curriculum matters to stand back from the prevailing views and institutions to critique them and to work to improve them. Do you agree? Do educational scholars and practitioners have a moral obligation to be critical of the ethics and justice of our educational system or should the scholar and practitioner be neutral?

Understanding How Curriculum Works in the Classroom

Not all curriculum research and scholarship is predominantly critical. In fact, much of it is aimed at solving practical problems and giving us a clear picture of how the curriculum actually works. Such scholar-researchers have to be inventive and creative problem solvers as they systematically collect empirical data, analyze it, and report their findings so that we can better understand what happens when we make and implement certain kinds of curriculum decisions. A good example of this form of scholarship can be found in the work of Swedish scholar Urban Dahllöf, who became concerned in the late 1960s with the effect of ability grouping on academic achievement. Swedish schools had been sharply divided at the upper secondary levels between practical and academic institutions, and the country was in the process of implementing educational reforms that would make Swedish secondary schools more like American comprehensive high schools. The question of whether to group students by ability within such schools was of intense practical concern to planners.

After reviewing existing studies of ability grouping, which found no significant differences between achievement test results for students taught in mixed-ability classes and those taught in ability-grouped classes, Dahllöf found himself dissatisfied with the tests used in the studies. He reanalyzed the results from three studies by sorting items from the achievement tests into categories corresponding to topics in the curriculum. He found that more test items were included for topics that appeared early in the curriculum, and hence would be covered early in the school year, and fewer test items for topics later in the curriculum. But, he reasoned, if students from ability-grouped classes were able to move through the course material at a faster rate, their advantage in test performance would come mainly on items near the end of the curriculum. So tests with few items covering material presented late in the year would not show this kind of an advantage.

He then analyzed the time spent by both types of classes on various parts of the curriculum. He discovered the high-ability classes spent less time on nearly all units than did classes of mixed ability. Hence, high-ability students in mixed-ability classes were moving through course material more slowly than their peers in ability-grouped classes. The data also showed a modest positive correlation between time spent on a given topic and scores on items covering that content. The finding of no difference between ability-grouped and mixed-ability classes was apparently the result of two canceling effects: in mixed-ability classes high-ability students spent more time on early units and thus scored slightly higher on those items than their peers in ability-grouped classes, whereas those students scored very much better on the few items covering topics at the end of the course. Result: no overall differences on these achievement tests!

These investigations led Dahllöf to construct a "macromodel for the curriculum process."[6] The central idea of the model is that, other things being equal, "the achievement level of a group of pupils in an achievement test of high content validity regarding a certain curriculum unit is a function of (1) general intelligence and initial achievement level of the group, (2) the level of the objective being tested (i.e., advanced, elementary, etc.) and (3) the time actually spent on learning the curriculum unit."[7] In traditional classroom instruction, the method of grouping youngsters determines the value of the first variable in his model. The other two variables are determined directly by the teacher but also indirectly by a variety of factors in the school environment that define and constrain the work of students and teachers, such as the school schedule, course syllabi, class size, length of school year, and so on. He called these latter factors "frame factors."

The teacher, acting within these frames, controlled students' time allotments to different curriculum units and the level of objectives that would be sought and expected. Dahllöf theorized that teachers set the pace of a class's progress through the course material by depending on the performance of some subset of the class. He guessed that this subset would be students achieving below the class average. He called this group the "criterion steering group." If students in the criterion steering group seemed ready to move on to the next curriculum unit, the teacher would move on. In high-ability classes, the steering group would be able to move at a faster pace than in mixed-ability classes where students in the criterion steering group would be lower in ability.

Dahllöf's model explains and generates testable hypotheses about curricular determinants of achievement. As a research scholar, he does not propose ability-grouped or mixed-ability classes, but rather suggests the trade-offs anyone must accept in choosing one or the other. Neither is completely superior in his analysis, but he has shown that each has its distinctive pattern of results for students of different abilities. The scholar's role, in this case, is to investigate, describe in detail, and illuminate the choices for us. It is a form of scholarship that leans heavily on the empirical, scientific model of research. It is not critical and judgmental, nor does it advocate courses of action. Empirical research is currently the dominant form of research in education. It aims to help us understand educational phenomena so that we may better predict, control, and make informed choices.

Curriculum in Relation to Culture

The forms of research and scholarship considered thus far in this chapter explain and criticize curriculum theory and practice from a relatively contemporary standpoint. When history is used by a critic, it is usually not his or her central concern. But historical research in its own right is another important form of curriculum scholarship. It helps us avoid reinventing the wheel. For instance, a look at the history of teaching reading will show that since the early nineteenth century there have been cyclical revivals of "alphabet" (phonetic) and "whole-word" (sight) approaches to the reading curriculum. Historical scholarship also helps us understand how the curriculum got to be what it is today. It gives us perspective over time. Historians are known for taking the long view of things, and our next example of curriculum scholarship takes a long view indeed.

Walter Ong, in *Rhetoric, Romance, and Technology*, considers a curious phenomenon in the history of Western education.[8] In ancient Greek and Roman civilization, in medieval monastery schools, in the first universities, and right up to the eighteenth century, the central subject of what we today call secondary and higher education was rhetoric. The precise mix of content included in this subject varied over the centuries, but it was always in the curriculum, and it dealt with the analysis of effective verbal communication, the logical analysis of arguments, effective techniques of persuasion, and the art of public speaking, among other things. Today such a course might be called "effective communication" or "using language effectively." Then, in the nineteenth century, with comparative suddenness, rhetoric fell from its preeminence and almost disappeared entirely from the curriculum of formal education. Why?

One theorizes that mastery of the dominant form of communication in one's time is an important determinant of a person's power in that culture. The subtitle of his book is, significantly, "studies in the interaction of expression and culture." Before the widespread introduction of printed material with the invention of movable type in the fifteenth century, Western cultures were based on oral traditions; speech was the dominant mode of expression. People who were taught as children to use speech skillfully could rise in power and position, within the limits permitted by the social structure. Those whose speech was ineffective found themselves with a considerable handicap. Such is also the case today, but even more so for those who cannot read.

Naturally, then, schools sought to prepare students to speak well. Classes in rhetoric could be expected to teach practical memory techniques—rhyming, rhythmic patterns, vivid imagery, mastery of common forms of argument and exposition. Students recited their lessons orally each day. They listened to great speeches recited from memory or read by their teachers. Students were taught to use "commonplaces"—lists of topics everyone expected to hear mentioned in connection with a given theme or on a given occasion. Our "who, what, when, where, why, how" is a modern holdover of the commonplace tradition.

Ong explains how this rhetorical tradition shaped Western literature and thought.

> Practice of one sort or another in the use of the commonplaces . . . helped
> with virtually all the poetry and other literature in the Western world from
> Homer through neoclassicism. This practice was a residue . . . of the oral
> heritage, which must place a premium on fixity.[9]

If speech is to be effective, it must be remembered by listeners. Rhetorical techniques emphasized the use of a fixed set of commonly expected forms so that the burden on what we today would call long-term memory was made manageable. "Any culture knows only what it can recall. An oral culture, by and large, could recall only what was held in mnemonically serviceable formulas."[10] What happened, then, to cause the abrupt decline of the teaching of rhetoric? Printing! When printing became widespread, ideas were no longer fleeting wisps that had to be caught and held in memory at first hearing and retransmitted orally at a later time. Both authors and readers could and did pause, reflect on a difficult passage, read it again, and study it—luxuries available earlier only to the privileged few who could afford handwritten manuscripts.

> When print locked information into exactly the same place upon the page
> in thousands of copies of the same book in type far more legible than any
> handwriting, knowledge came suddenly to the fingertips. With knowledge
> fastened down in visually processed space, man acquired an intellectual
> security never known before.[11]

When visual print became the dominant mode of expression, the educational relevance of oral rhetoric disappeared. The oral recitation came to be seen as old-fashioned and was soon replaced by textbooks, blackboards, paper, pen, and ink—the tools of literacy. Memorization declined in importance, while mass instruction in reading and writing grew. Emphasis on the sound of language, on figures of speech, and on other essentially oral characteristics was replaced by emphasis on its content and written form.

Ong's explanation, and others like it, calls our attention to the great waves of historical change that may pass almost unnoticed in one person's lifetime but that profoundly shape the development of the curriculum across several generations. Think of our current age and the advent of computers. Information is being stored not in print, but in electronic form on disks and tapes that cannot be read, as a book can, without a machine. "Writing" is being done by word processors, and just as the advent of printing required the invention of special marks to signal in print such oral things as pauses (comma), emphasis (exclamation point), and a new thought (paragraph indentation), so, too, electronic cursors move to command functions and new "marks" are invented and stored electronically as our text is being formed and made ready for retrieval. Think, too, of "electronic mail," of "bulletin boards," of "menus" to software, and of creating your own "program." Even these common words take on different meanings in this new mode of expression. If Ong's form of explanation is correct and if the new information technology is producing a revolution in the fundamental way we express ourselves, what changes would you predict for the curriculum of schools in the next century?

The forms of scholarly explanation and critique that we have considered in this chapter do not tell us what the curriculum should be or how we should determine what it should be. We have seen a scholarly critique of a theory, a moral critique of a theory, a moral critique of society and the school as a social instrument, a scientific explanation of the relation of achievement to ability groupings, and a historical explanation of curriculum and the dominant form of cultural expression. Many people would see these and other scholarly works in educational research as "ivory tower," impractical, theoretical—of little direct use to the practitioner. But we believe that they can be extremely helpful. John Maynard Keynes, the British economist, is supposed to have said "there's nothing as practical as a good theory." Upon reflection, it is easy to see the practical value of a theoretical critique of current practice, even if it leaves us without a better alternative. It makes us aware of potential problems and how we may be able to avoid them. It challenges us to search for practices not subject to the same criticisms. Even though theories that explain curriculum phenomena do not tell us what to do, they can help us decide by giving us a clearer and deeper understanding of what is involved in the decision and what may be the consequences of the actions we are considering. Scholarship provides perspective.

But *using* these theories demands more from us. We must ourselves infer what actions to take that would moot the criticism or use to advantage the principles put forward in the explanation. The reasoning involved can be arduous mental labor. Worse, it may be impossible to know if we have done it right. Can you be certain you know what to do now that you understand Ong's principle that schools teach the dominant mode of expression? Should we stop teaching reading and writing, as we have largely stopped teaching rhetoric? Should we add "media studies" to the curriculum? Life would certainly be easier for us if Ong had given us a theory that told us what to teach or one that told us exactly how to go about determining this, instead of explaining one principle relating curriculum to culture. Still, his view gives us perspective. What, if anything, might be gained from the other explanations and criticisms described in this chapter?

We believe that only by seeing more deeply into the nature of things are we able to deal more wisely with them, morally assess them, fully and fairly judge them, and shape them to our purposes. The traditional Western ideal of an educated person is one for whom the unexamined life is not worth living. We believe that professional educators cannot let an important part of their professional lives go unexamined and still think of themselves as educated. The literature of critical scholarly research provides them with an important resource. Before going on you might want to examine the case "The Teacher as Critic" and the dispute "Theory and Practice," in chapter 8.

Chapter 7

Finding a Balance

Thus far, and even in our chapter on "The Aims of Education," we have paid little attention to who was doing the aiming for education. The implicit assumption, more often than not, was that some one entity, some single-minded agent, was stating, choosing, using, or evaluating aims. In some cases this individual turned out to be a philosopher defining, justifying, and reasoning about aims; in others it was a curriculum specialist, a teacher, or an administrator who was stating aims and seeking ways to reach them. Following the prevailing practice in contemporary curriculum theory, we said nothing about what to do when, in real life, people do not agree about aims, when the aims proposed apply to a whole school or school system that serves a diverse and pluralistic community in an open, democratic society.

What happens when people disagree about aims, or about the priority among them? Does it make sense to speak of a school's aims, a community's aims, or a society's aims? If we speak in these ways, what happens to the aims of those individuals who may not share the aims of others in a school, in a community, or in a society? What can we do, as professionals, when confronted, as we no doubt will be, with conflict over aims? These questions will be our concern in this chapter.

Lack of Consensus

Most educators and citizens seem to think that if only they had a clear idea of the ends they were seeking and their priorities among them, then our curriculum problems could be posed in a straightforward way and solutions sought through routine, systematic methods. This kind of thinking has been called "technical rationality" by Jürgen Habermas, by which he means the seeking of means-ends solutions to our problems.[1] Tyler's rationale and its many variations exemplify the technical-rational approach to curriculum making. First aims and objectives are determined, and then means are designed to achieve them. It is assumed that consensus on the aims of education can be reached without serious problems. Yet the evidence indicates that controversy is at least as common as consensus. The truly difficult curriculum problems require us to proceed in the face of disagreement about the aims of education. Let us look at some of the evidence about agreement and disagreement on the aims of education.

Every year since 1965 the Gallup organization has conducted a poll of American public opinion about education. Reading the results of these polls gives one the strong impression that there are diverse opinions and priorities among the American public regarding the aims of education. In the fourth such poll, in 1969, for example, respondents were asked this question: "People have different reasons why they want their children to get an education. What are the chief reasons that come to your mind?" The results, expressed in percentages of respondents mentioning each in some way or other, were as follows:

1. To get better jobs   44%
2. To get along better with people at all levels of society   43%
3. To make more money and to achieve financial success   38%
4. To attain self-satisfaction   21%
5. To stimulate their minds   15%
6. Miscellaneous reasons   11%[2]

These responses hardly show a consensus about aims.

In the same survey, respondents were asked this question: "Which three of these educational programs would you like your local . . . schools to give *more attention* to?" The top three ranked program goals were:

1. Teaching students to respect law and authority
2. Teaching students how to solve problems and think for themselves
3. Teaching students vocational skills[3]

In the more recent 1985 Gallup poll of "Teachers Attitudes Toward the Public Schools, Part 2," a comparison was presented between U.S. teachers' and the public's views on "the goals of education."[4] A list of twenty-five goals was provided to those being polled. They were to rank each on a scale of 0 (not at all important) to 10 (the most important goal). Percentages represent the proportion of teachers and the public giving a particular goal a 10. Because one could give a score of 10 to more than one goal, percentages do not add up to 100. Among the teachers, five goals were ranked highest by 51–56 percent of the respondents:

1. Developing good work habits   56%
2. Developing the ability to think   56%

3. Developing the ability to speak and write correctly   55%
4. Developing the ability to use math   53%
5. Encouraging the desire for learning   51%

While 68 percent of the public agreed with the teachers about their third-ranked goal of the importance of learning to speak and write correctly, 64 percent (vs. 33 percent of the teachers) gave highest priority to "developing standards of what's right and wrong." Of the public, 54 percent (vs. 34 percent of the teachers) thought it was most important to help students not planning to go to college to develop skills needed for getting jobs, and 46 percent (vs. 28 percent of the teachers) saw as most important students' learning about "sex, marriage, parenting, personal finances, alcohol, and drug abuse."[5]

Clearly, American educators and the public value many diverse educational aims and do not seem to agree on priorities. Some place a higher value on one sort of aim than another, but a list that would encompass all the important aims of all segments of the American public and its educators would need to include a great variety of items. The evidence of these recent polls does not support the idea of a popular consensus on the aims of American education.

The history of American education, of the actual choices made by Americans through their leaders and their institutions, also reveals a record of lurches and pendulum swings in various directions—toward Americanization when immigration seemed to threaten American ways, toward inculcation of democratic values when totalitarianism threatened, toward scientific and technical excellence when the public was concerned about our military and economic power, toward equality of educational opportunity when social divisions erupted in violence, toward career education and basic skills when unemployment rose. These lurches and swings are superimposed on a steady trend of expansion (of numbers of students, teachers, schools, subjects, dollars) and broadening (more comprehensive programs, more tasks assigned to the school, an increasing variety of expectations). The history of American education hardly can be said to support any consensus on aims for education, unless it is the whole set of all aims ever seriously proposed.

The fact is that no substantial agreement exists among philosophers, the public, or the profession on what should be the aims of a general education for all. The illusion of consensus is fostered by high-sounding abstractions like "educating each child to its fullest potential," "equity and excellence," and "building a democratic society." We go for years at a stretch without educational controversy breaking into the headlines, and sometimes a temporary unity is created by some event that galvanizes public concern, as with Sputnik; but the substantial and continuing consensus that is presupposed by curriculum theories about procedures that begin "first, determine your aims clearly and specifically" is a rare event, not the usual state of affairs.

Lack of consensus and controversy over the aims of education, having continued for centuries, are likely to be with us permanently. Clearly, teachers, administrators, and curriculum makers need strategies for coping with disagreements about aims.

How do we proceed with curriculum making when people do not agree on aims?

Technical-Rational Procedures

The dominant response of those who advocate technical-rational procedures of curriculum making that require clear statements of objectives has been to try to find support for aims and objectives by means of empirical methods. In this way, technical-rational methods, like Tyler's, claim to be more scientific than other methods in common use. To live up to its professed ideals, therefore, technical-rational curriculum making seeks a form of objective justification of specific aims as well as scientific methods for pursuing them. Three fundamental strategies have been proposed for reaching objective agreement on specific aims as a preliminary to scientific curriculum making: rational argument, scientific investigation, and voting or polling. These can be combined, and often are, in a process called "needs assessment." Let us consider them in their pure forms.

As we have seen, Tyler emphasizes the importance of developing a "philosophy of education," a general statement of the fundamental beliefs and values about education shared by the community of people associated with a school. By debating the contents of such a general statement, the community expresses its basic values and, it is hoped, reflects a general consensus. Rational arguments can then be framed that justify *specific* objectives in terms of this philosophy. However, rational argument, important as it is, is seen by many as a "prescientific" method. They believe that one of the great contributions of science to intellectual life has been its demonstration of the advantages of disciplining pure reason by making it operate on evidence derived from careful observations and experiments. Otherwise, pure reason can tend toward a casuistry that occupies us with debates over unresolvable issues, such as how many angels can fit on the head of a pin, or may lead us to a hopeless relativism in which plausible and logically consistent arguments can be advanced for any coherent set of propositions. Therefore, advocates of "scientific curriculum making" seek methods for justifying aims that go beyond rational argument to employ more scientific methods, such as observation and experiment, in the support of specific aims and objectives.

Simple factual information can often provide strong empirical justification for adopting an educational objective, given very general value agreement. Tyler frequently uses health education as an example of this. By collecting statistics on the incidence of various health problems in the community, it would be possible to establish the community's health education needs objectively. All that is required initially is some general agreement in the community about some global value regarding health, such as "the alleviation of human misery is a good thing," and then specific aims and objectives in line with this value can be determined. For example, a communicable disease that could be prevented through better sanitation suggests the objective of teaching better personal sanitation habits. A high incidence of dental cavities and gum disease suggests teaching good dental hygiene. The misery caused by accidents, stress-related disorders, and chronic disabilities affected by diet and exercise could be reduced or prevented by appropriate health education. Holding the global value of "alleviation of human misery" provides a potential source for determining quite specific educational aims or objectives by means of collecting relevant information.

Thus, "scientific" curriculum makers believe that factual evidence based on careful observation provides much more convincing justification for accepted educational aims than reasoning based upon unsupported assumptions, and they also believe that even more convincing support is possible through experimentation. We can illustrate this methodology with the following example. Suppose someone tried an experiment in which many communities were observed for a long period of time. In some of these, a health education program would be implemented, using facts about the main health problems in each. In the remaining communities, similar facts would be collected about the incidence of health problems, but no intervention would be made via the health education offered by the schools. If, after ten or twenty years, the incidence of the identified health problems was lower in those communities whose schools used the experimental health education program as compared with the other communities, the benefits to community health of pursuing the health education objectives would have been demonstrated more convincingly than any simple collection of facts could do. Such studies are generally referred to as evaluation studies.

The hope of scientific curriculum making is that, taken together, the combination of rational argument and scientific evidence can build such a strong case for certain aims and programs that disagreements about aims can be resolved. Sometimes this happens, but not always. Furthermore, these methods are so time consuming and expensive that we could not afford to determine specific needs or resolve all disputes about aims this way, even if we could in principle do so. And some would argue that, in principle, it is not possible to settle questions about aims in these ways.

Another method sometimes advocated is simply to poll those affected and adopt the aims endorsed by a majority. This method would permit us to determine that our educational aims at least have the support of most of those concerned. However, it assumes that people generally know their own minds and look out for their own best interests, and that any aim endorsed by a majority of the community has a strong claim to support by the school. These are challengeable assumptions, especially the last one. Nevertheless, if we were to adopt only those aims supported by an over-whelming majority, we would at least seem to be able to steer clear of cases where controversy is likely to be greatest and most disabling, and thus ensure that we attend to the aims favored by most of our constitu-ents. For some purposes, this is enough justification to move forward with more systematic, "scientific" methods of curriculum making. However, as we have already seen in our look at the Gallup polls, seldom do any aims get more than 50–60 percent of the public's "vote," and various multiple aims and goals are given high priority by different groups. Before going on, you might want to consider a situation of multiple goals in the case "One School's Philosophy of Education," in chapter 8.

Searching for Balance Among Contending Aims

One way to mitigate the effects of dissent on aims, and thus reach some-thing like a working consensus, is to try to keep a balance among the contending aims. We believe this is a better way to proceed. To do this one must first overcome the idea that education has an aim, only one aim, and recognize the fact that people have many aims and many good reasons for having them. Then, even when one major aim is dominant, for whatever reasons, the others still can be preserved from complete neglect. Conflict among proponents of different aims can be limited by emphasizing in various ways the undeniable claims that each aim has to be a legitimate part of the full spectrum of aims. One also needs to recognize that priori-ties need to change over time in response to changing conditions and emerging hopes and values.

The intellectual basis for seeking such a balance among aims, there-fore, is a conception of the aims of education that is not monolithic, but that has room for some diversity and multiplicity as well as responsive-ness to new conditions and emerging social values. We already alluded to a way to categorize aims in a very basic and all-encompassing heuristic way when we contrasted subject-, student-, and society-centered perspec-tives of curriculum. In its simplest terms, our conception requires that education needs to seek a functional equilibrium among the sometimes competing demands of these three basic educational aims: to cultivate knowledge, to sustain and improve the society, and to foster the well-being of individuals. We believe that each of these is a legitimate and primary concern of a major segment of the population and that everyone should recognize that each is important to some degree in all education. If any one of these three important educational tasks were neglected for a long time, serious troubles surely would follow.

Yet it is never completely clear what the priorities should be among these three overarching educational tasks. When we seek ways to accomplish them all within the same program, we seem never to be completely successful, and we disagree about what compromises to make. Thus, we have the basis for a measure of consensus but also a high probability of continued disagreement. There also is no doubt that sometimes these general aims are in direct conflict and opposition. Success comes, however, not when one side wins, but when we have enough consensus to support viable educational programs regarding a balance of these aims and enough dissent to power continued adaptation to changing circumstances.

The real curriculum problem, then, becomes how to proceed when aims and priorities are unstable and shifting, how to maintain a sound and effective educational program that is at the same time open to changes in its aims and priorities. This is more a practical and political problem than a philosophical or technical-rational one. In a sense, the philosophical problem of determining the aims of education has been "solved"—not eliminated once and for all, but made more comprehensible and put in a form in which it can be approached by other means. In our view, the grand aims of education have been determined. We should aim at the transmission of knowledge, the good of society, and the good life for the individual. When these aims are or seem to be in conflict with one another, the real question is, is there any way to proceed to accommodate diversity and contention about aims?

Political Aiming

As we have seen, polling as a method of aim determination moves us from attempts to reconcile differences by rational-scientific means to attempts based on the exercise of some form of power, in this case the power of the majority. We speak of such methods as being *political*, using the term in a broad sense to mean attempts to deal with and reconcile our practical interests and to find ways of living together in harmony. In a democratic society, the will of the majority, as expressed in voting or polling, is taken as a legitimate basis for an official state agency's exercise of power. For example, dissenting individuals may be forced to comply with policies they may not favor but that have been enacted by legitimate institutions. However, polling does not provide an opportunity for discussion, debate, deliberation, compromise, and accommodation. And these are needed if our practical interests are to be served effectively in the political arena.

Of course, all that is really necessary for public education to operate effectively is for those who dissent from a policy not to interfere with its execution. A true consensus supporting the policy is not necessary. Parties without enough power or influence may tolerate a situation not wholly to their liking if the costs and risks of fighting it are too great. Sometimes they can bargain with more powerful groups and agree to tolerate some troubling policies if others that are more important to them are corrected. Informal bargains of this sort are often struck when parties are evenly matched or when many small groups contend and no one has enough power to dominate the others. All parties realize they lack the power to get their way, and all crave some resolution of the conflict, so they bargain.

In fact, most of the significant curriculum issues in American education have been resolved through political battles in one locality after another, usually accompanied by national debate and national attention. Very few, if any, have been solved by technical-rational procedures. For example, around the turn of this century the importance of the classics in colleges and in secondary education was hotly debated by academics and the public, as we have seen in our treatment of progressives and traditionalists. The question of including Darwin's theories of evolution in high school curricula was also debated in many state legislatures in the early decades of this century, and many states enacted laws forbidding the teaching of these ideas. The Scopes trial in Tennessee was part of the long-drawn-out political process of resolving, for a time, this curricular dispute, which resurfaced with the "creationist" lawsuits in the 1980s. Similar battles were fought in courts and legislatures over the issue of vocational education. Even subjects as apparently innocuous as mathematics and reading became centers of controversy that were resolved by political means. The same is true of temperance, drugs, and sex education. It seems that just about every major curriculum reform has ridden on the back of a political campaign on its behalf in state capitals and in local boards of education, as well as in the media and in Washington, D.C. And most of them have experienced political opposition, too, at one point or another in their history.

It should be clear that rational-scientific and political methods of conflict resolution are quite different. One invokes a cool, dispassionate, objective approach to settling differences; the other demands passionate caring for values and ideals and recognizes the importance of dialogue, struggle, negotiation, and the political process of accommodation. In our modern professional and technical educational establishment, rational-scientific methods predominate. After all, we expect physicians to decide about treatments on the basis of solid scientific evidence and not on the preferences of their patients or debates with other doctors. So we also expect professional educators to decide issues by using their expertise and skill in the scientific-rational processes that underlie professional practice. We expect professionals to use their best informed judgment in serving their clients' interests. However, these expectations are not met in a political process where power may be distributed according to majority, wealth, family connections, longevity, or personal qualities other than professional competence, or one where people's decisions represent their own interests or those of their reference group rather than the interests of all their clients.

Many educators are understandably nervous at the thought that the aims and content of education might be established through some political process, rather than by objective methods and the best judgment of qualified professionals. Many professional educators today are disheartened by the succession of demands emanating from the public for educational emphases that seem contradictory. By the time the profession has begun to respond to them, they are confronted with a new set of criticisms and new demands for still other reforms.

On the other hand, our democratic ideals suggest that every citizen has a right to a voice in determining important matters of public policy. Citizens feel frustrated at being unable to effect lasting school reforms even in times of national crisis when the public seems united. Everyone seems profoundly dissatisfied. The situation is unstable, and the institutions of public education threaten either to collapse or to harden into self-defensive rigidity.

We have here a conflict between our commitment to rational-scientific procedures and our commitment to the principle of democratic governance. We feel that curriculum decisions should reflect both, yet the two do not always agree. We urgently need ways for determining aims and policies for education that can accommodate diversity of interest and opinion while still resting on a firm foundation of objective knowledge; and this must be done over time in changing contexts. As we have seen, agreement on the aims of education is not as routine or as easy to come by as the technical-rational approach assumes it is. Therefore, we believe that the political process must be given a much more prominent place in education than it is traditionally given in technical-rational forms of curriculum theory.

In order to do this, we will need a large-scale, long-term approach to public policy that reconciles democracy and science in the most numerous, the most basic, and the most important cases, even where only a limited accommodation can be reached on educational aims, policies, and programs. Some form of *participative social planning* appears to be required. We believe that the political and the technical cannot be neatly divided the way the technical-rational procedures require. Each must interact throughout the planning process—from the identification of people's discontents and formulation of rough ideas of what might clear them up, to the identification of important aims and needs and the design of operational programs. Debate on the merits of competing designs for policies, programs, and practices to achieve certain aims becomes more pointed and more useful than debate on aims or objectives alone. And revision of designs offers a greater potential for compromises than does the mere rewriting of aim statements. Our practical and our technical interests need to be served in unison.

We have seen that curriculum theories based on aims are designed to enable experts to develop procedures for accomplishing well-defined educational results. Participative social planning will have to be designed to enable both experts and the public to determine jointly, over an extended period of time, the shape of educational programs and policies. The public will also need to learn to think more deeply, fully, and fairly about curriculum and aims, as you have done in this book.

A Plan for Action

How is all this to be accomplished? It will not be easy; it will require good will on the part of the participants; it will also require a carefully thought-out set of institutional arrangements. We can only suggest how it might be done here by means of an imaginary example. The difficult technical-rational job of devising some means to reach our practical end of living together in harmony and seeking the good of all will still have to be done, and it may not look like our imaginary solution at all. But we are convinced that the practical, the political, and the technical-rational must be merged in some way. Here are our thoughts on the matter. Can you think of a better way?

Imagine that a National Educational Policies Commission were to be created, and that this commission was composed of twenty or so members, some representing professional interests such as the National Education Association, American Federation of Teachers, and chief state school officers and others representing lay interests—parents, taxpayers, students, and business, labor, and civic groups.

Imagine that this commission sponsored inquiries into the educational needs of groups, of individuals, and of the nation; that it asked for contending briefs from various parties commenting on the various needs proposed; that it held forums where the representatives of these various views could question one another; and that these hearings could culminate in the publication by the commission of recommended actions for legislatures, the U.S. Office of Education, the National Institute of Education, and other responsible agencies, or of recommendations for further study to clarify remaining points of contention, or of popular versions of the debates that could be used as a spur to discussion among the general public of the issues raised. The force of such recommendations would doubtless be great, but it would be moral force, not direct federal power.

Imagine that this commission established standing committees to focus on the special problems of certain populations—the poor, children in rural areas, the handicapped child, and so on. Imagine that these standing committees also reported periodically to the parent commission on the special characteristics and needs of these populations. And imagine that these reports, too, were examined critically with the aid of explicit adversarial procedures.

Imagine that this commission periodically invited various defenders and critics of particular major features of schools to prepare contending briefs for careful restudy. For example, reports could be invited every seven to ten years on science in public education, during which those concerned about science—professional associations, science teachers, representatives from business and industry, scientists themselves, anti-evolutionists, anti-scientists, and so on—could all be invited to be heard, perhaps in a series of regional forums culminating in a major national debate and a series of commission recommendations.

Imagine that careful studies—historical, philosophical, psychological, sociological—were also commissioned during and subsequent to these debates in hope of settling some issues that seem to rest on a contended matter of fact or theory or in hope of stimulating further ideas where current ones seem inadequate.

Imagine that states also established similar commissions to carry on similar activities in areas of particular concern to the citizens of that state and to determine how best to act on the recommendations of the national commission.

Imagine that states placed a mandatory expiration date of no more than ten years on all legislation and administrative regulations that required course or program elements for elementary and secondary schools, so that the responsible body would have to renew that requirement by formal action or let it lapse.

Imagine that local schools could appeal to the state commission any

requirement placed upon them by the state board or department of education and be entitled to a hearing before that commission in which the
responsible state agency would have to defend its actions against that
challenge.

Imagine that local schools could, with the concurrence of local parents,
submit their own indicators of what they were accomplishing to the state
authorities, in addition to whatever statewide indicators were imposed
upon them. Imagine that these indicators themselves were made the subject of intensive study and negotiation among the various interests—professional and lay—in the state.

Imagine that those districts found by the state to be failing to perform
up to par on the state's indicators were asked to present their case before
the state board or state commission, with the state's representatives to
present the other side.

Imagine that local teachers, administrators, and parents could make
depositions detailing their reactions of support or opposition to any state
policy or practice to the state board and that the board would, after inves-
tigating the matter, either publish its official opinion or authorize formal
public hearings on the situation.

Imagine that any group of twenty or more students, with their parents'
support, who wished to substitute some course or other program element
not now available for one now required could petition to this effect by
signature and by showing that the service could be provided at a cost to
the district no greater than the pro-rated cost of the required course.
Imagine that the district, in ruling on this petition, had to offer a public
rationale for its decision and that the petitioner could appeal this decision
to a county or state board. On appeal, the local schools and the state
agency responsible for the requirement would be expected to defend their
actions and dispute the claims by those wishing to substitute for their
requirements.

These ideas are but fragments. Important objections could be made to
each, and each valid objection would require some sort of precaution if
any such set of institutional arrangements were to be made workable. But
building a workable set of such arrangements for participatory social planning, development, and execution of our curriculum and aims should, in
our estimation, be one of the most important items on the agenda of
American education.

Since midcentury, educational scholars and researchers seem to have
shied away from the public problems of determining aims and objectives,
setting priorities, establishing and defending basic purposes for education. Purposes seem to be beyond our science-minded, technically oriented professionals. Ends, aims, goals, and the like have been relegated to

the status of irrational human longings or subjective value judgments. Even philosophers have denied that their discipline allows them to say anything distinctive about the ends of education.[6]

As a result, most scholarly treatments of aims assume away one of their most fundamental characteristics: the prevalence of disagreement about aims that we have highlighted in this chapter. Researchers all too often have assumed that somewhere there are explicit objectives that it is someone's duty (usually the practitioners' or laypeople's) to state explicitly so that they can get on with their scientific work. Such attitudes leave the practitioner with nothing to rely on except hunches and intuition, and they leave the researcher with a "science" built upon the shifting sands of opinion.

In fits and starts, in lurches and pendulum swings, we strive for intellectual resolution of disagreements about aims but seldom succeed in building a consensus of belief. We try to build more and more comprehensive educational institutions, ministering to an ever-increasing list of aims, in an effort to permit simultaneous pursuit of divergent goals in a spirit of tolerance; but we run the risk of aimlessness in the process. We intermittently and not very systematically engage in extensive discussions of educational issues and elaborate procedural rituals, seeking working accommodations among differing views and interests; but these are often fragile and fleeting. Sometimes we retreat in frustration to the more manageable job of determining aims for mathematics, language teaching, or some other compartment of general education, hoping that if everyone handles their part well, the whole enterprise will come out well. We believe that we should do more.

It would be so nice, would it not, if somewhere we could discover the true aims of education. But in the final analysis, there is no final analysis. We are stuck with the uncertainty of pursuing aims that will shift and change in our open democratic setting. However, we believe that through some institutionalized form of participatory social planning, we as professional educators can expend our best efforts to propose aims, critically examine them, join with others in full and fair deliberation about them, exercise our best judgment, individually and collectively, and pursue our chosen aims with energy, intelligence, and a tolerance of others who emerge from the same process with different conclusions. The professional literature in education is a vital aid in this process, enabling educators and the public to benefit from the extended dialogue among articulate practitioners, scholars, and researchers.

And so we arrive at the bittersweet conclusion that, although there are no firm conclusions about the curriculum and aims of education, there is much to be learned from studying and thinking about them. Our hopes lie in the continual progress of our understanding and the reaching of reasonable accommodations, rather than in the finding of final solutions. The last debate in chapter 8, "Whose Aims Matter?," invites you to consider what this conception of curriculum and aims may mean to you as a professional educator.

Chapter 8

Cases and Disputes

To this point we have considered a number of ways to think about curriculum and aims, and we have asked you to think about them along the way. Through the cases and disputes in this chapter, we hope to bring theory and practice, thinking and acting, closer together. We also hope to bring some of the complexity of the real world of education into view, because it is there that thinking, decision making, and acting responsibly need to be done.

To help you understand and use the perspectives on curriculum and aims we have offered in this book, in this last chapter we provide a set of realistic vignettes in the form of cases, dialogues, and disputes that raise a number of issues not dealt with directly or at length in the text. As you read them, think about the issues embedded in them and discuss them with others. We think you will see why being able to think about curriculum and aims in a variety of basic ways can make a difference in how teachers and administrators act. We think you will also see that we have not been dealing with esoteric theoretical ideas that have no relation to practice.

The cases and disputes that follow clearly show that the individual and collective curriculum practices of educators, yourself included, can and do have lasting effects on the lives of persons and on the society in which we all live. As professional educators, we believe that we all have a responsibility to consider, monitor, and when morally appropriate, alter those effects. These cases and disputes are designed to help you become more sensitive to this obligation of responsible professional educators.

To give you an overview of the topics we have treated and the major points at issue in them, we have provided a summary (see table 1) from which you can select cases and disputes of special interest to you. Of course, we could neither treat all the possible topics and issues that now exist nor anticipate those that would be of central concern when you are using this text. So you should feel free to write your own cases and disputes or to bring issues from your own experience into your class discussions.

Some of you may already have sampled these cases and disputes

TABLE 1. Summary of Cases and Disputes

Page	Title*	Central Issue
93	Curriculum Change (1)	Does curriculum change require teacher commitment?
94	Freedom and Learning (2)	What should be done when ideal aims and reality clash?
95	Education for Life (2)	Does a progressive or a traditional curriculum best prepare one for life?
97	Workforce School (2)	Might an effective currculum limit vocational opportunities?
98	Individual Differences and Equality of Opportunity (3)	Is what is good for society good for the individual?
99	Mass or Class Culture? (3)	Does popular culture have a place in the curriculum?
100	National Reports on Education (3)	Should the curriculum serve perceived national needs?
101	Go Fly a Kite (3)	Do different conceptions of the same subject matter produce different learnings?
103	Individualized Learning (4)	Should there be a curriculum for each child?
104	Grading Policies (4)	Are grading policies and curriculum conceptions connected?
105	A Social Studies Curriculum (4)	Which conceptualization of curriculum is most useful to teachers?
106	To Each His Own (5)	Is local control of curriculum a myth or reality?
108	The Geometry Curriculum (5)	Do textbooks or aims determine a teacher's curriculum?
109	Do Procedures Make a Difference? (5)	Are curriculum-making procedures biased?
110	Teaching "Relevant" Literature (5)	What is the place of situational factors in curriculum making?
111	The Teacher as Critic (6)	What is the place of educational research in practical affairs?
112	Theory and Practice (6)	What is the relation of theory to practice?
113	One School's Philosophy of Education (7)	Should all teachers in a school agree on a philosophy of education?
114	Whose Aims Matter? (7)	How should disagreements about aims be handled?

*A number in parentheses after a title indicates that the case or dispute is recommended for use with that specific chapter.

when following the suggestions we made in each chapter. To indicate our recommendations as to the relation of issues to specific chapters, we have placed a chapter number in parentheses following the title of each case or dispute listed. Of course, you should feel free to use them in any order suitable to your interests and purposes.

Curriculum Change

Susan Chin taught German at Bailey High, a large public high school. Susan had been teaching at Bailey for two years and felt things were going well. She liked her job. The students were learning. She enjoyed them. And she enjoyed working with Max Schmidt, the other member of the German department. Max had been teaching for twelve years; Susan respected Max's advice, and he was always happy to lend a hand.

One day in August, before the new school year was to start, Max came to Susan's room with a proposal for redesigning the German language curriculum. He talked about the recent national report on foreign language teaching and the finding that after graduation most students were unable to converse fluently in the language they had studied. Max explained that during the summer he had attended a workshop for language teachers in which a very different teaching method was demonstrated. This method stressed immersion in the language and rapid-fire give and take between teacher and student. The idea was that the language was to become second nature to the students. They were actually to think in the language, not think of responses in English and then mentally translate; hence the rapid exchange in which there would not be time to ponder. Lessons from texts with their grammar exercises and vocabulary lists were to take a minor place. This was a reversal of the general patterns that Max and Susan had used up to that time.

Max was very enthusiastic about the new curriculum and told Susan he was going to institute it in his classes and that she ought to also, not only because it was a superior method but because it would be best for the students if there was consistency in the German language program.

In thinking the matter over after Max had gone, Susan was uneasy. The new curriculum sounded interesting, but Susan could not generate strong feelings about it one way or the other. She had always included conversation in her classes. By and large, her students had done quite well. So she did not see any real point in changing her curriculum. On the other hand, she could not raise any real objections to the new program Max suggested. She had not been involved in the workshop, but Max certainly would take the time to explain the materials and procedures to her. She was fairly sure she could handle the new technique, although it did not really fit her style of teaching, which was rather more restrained than Max's. Plus, Max was so enthusiastic about the new program, and his judgment had always been sound before. Susan did not see how she could say no without any really good reasons. Besides, he had more seniority. Susan wished she could put more thought into the matter, but time was getting short, school would start soon, and plans had to be made. What should she do?

Should Susan go along with Max's plan? What positive and negative things might result from her compliance? From her refusal? Are there other options open to Susan? What would you do if you were Susan? How would you explain your position to Max? Must a teacher rationalize and be committed to the curriculum he or she teaches?

Freedom and Learning

The Hillsdale Alternative High School has been operating for ten years now. Its basic philosophy is still based on the principles of freedom and participatory self-determination. At the beginning of each academic year, the school community—teachers, students, and concerned parents—meets to review and revamp the curriculum as needed and to seek agreement on maxims for conduct, on an acceptable grading system, and on procedures for handling social and academic problems.

Max Ritter, who had taught social studies at the regular high school for five years, was pleased that his request for transfer to the "A" school had been approved. He firmly believed that an atmosphere of freedom and self-determination was conducive to genuine and meaningful learning. He soon had reason to doubt his basic beliefs, however.

During the first week of school the initial community "curriculum and school rules" meeting went well enough. A nice mix of standard subjects and some exotic courses was approved. It was also agreed that class attendance would be voluntary, grading would be pass/fail, and only very serious academic or social problems would be brought before the student-parent-faculty governing board. With the pettiness of rules put aside, the threat of competitive grading eliminated, and free choice of subjects instituted, Max felt that the best ground had been laid for meaningful learning and that it would be a great year for him and for his students.

Two months into the term, however, things at Hillsdale "A" did not seem to be working out well. Students often preferred to sunbathe in the courtyard instead of attending classes. Many had only chosen the exotic courses. In the regular courses Max taught, few prepared for class, figuring a spurt at the end would probably net them a passing grade. Consequently, classes were hard to teach, because no one had done the homework. Serious students and most teachers, including Max, became frustrated. Parents who expected their children to go to college complained. Max wondered if he had made a wrong move asking to transfer to Hillsdale "A" school. Things seemed out of hand.

Another community meeting was called to address the situation, now recognized as a serious problem that might call for a reconsideration and a new beginning. Many of the veteran "A"-school teachers spoke on the values of freedom for individual growth and of learning to take responsibility for one's choices and decisions. They argued that this year's experience would be a good lesson for next year's classes. But many parents objected that if things were allowed to continue under this year's rules, their children would lose a year and graduating seniors might not get into college. To the surprise of many, a number of students, who admitted they had enjoyed their freedom, now complained of boredom, lack of discipline, and lack of structure in lessons and curriculum. They wanted reform. Others wanted things to stay the way they were, because they were having a great time and wanted their initial "contract" to be honored.

A new teacher stood up and offered a solution. She argued that it was time to be rational about freedom and self-determination. "When these principles do harm, they are not good," she said. She suggested ways to restrict the realm of free choice for students, to set up an objective grading system, to establish a more demanding curriculum, and to enforce stricter standards of behavior.

Max surprised himself when he got to his feet and shouted, "But that would undermine the basic philosophy of the school!" Redfaced and confused, he sat down and watched as it seemed that no agreement would be reached.

Make up your own ending to this case. (Role playing parts of students, teachers, and parents might help raise some basic issues.) Should the community try to maintain their basic commitment to freedom or restrict it to ensure optimal learning? Can freedom be made a basis for learning without also being a potential basis for anarchy? Is the Hillsdale "A" school more Rouseauian or Deweyan?

Education for Life

P: If we have learned anything from the past, it's that we cannot predict the future. Before the twentieth century, splitting the atom was considered impossible and no one could possibly have anticipated the problems of nuclear waste or nuclear war. Therefore, educators cannot be content to teach what we think we now know. We must prepare people for the future by teaching them how to think and how to solve problems.

T: Problem solving is important, of course, and the future can't be known, that's true. But I believe that the best way to be prepared to face the future is with a rich knowledge of what human beings have come to know about themselves and their world and not just with some skills of critical thinking. In fact, critical thinking is best taught through a study of science, philosophy, and even art. These critical ways of thinking that are imbedded in our cultural heritage must be passed on by teaching these subjects.

P: No, critical thinking and problem-solving skills are best learned not through books and lectures on traditional subjects, but through experiment and successful adaptations in real-life situations. Too much of schooling is a pedantic worshiping of traditions removed from the real world. No wonder students see little connection between life and what they learn in school. We must make learning meaningful, and that can only happen if people are not forced to study things disconnected from their lives, but given the opportunity to study what interests them.

T: But students are too young to know what's meaningful. We adults are better judges of what will be the rich rewards of a solid classical education. Interests can be fickle in youth. What's relevant today may not be so tomorrow. The wisdom of the past is always relevant.

P: Let's get down to brass tacks! What butcher or barber needs to know algebra or physics? What banker or shopkeeper needs chemistry or ancient history? What policeman, Shakespeare; or nurse, philosophy? What ordinary people need to know is how to solve real problems, how to be good workers, good parents, and good citizens. Your education is for an elite, not for good, ordinary people.

T: You are so shortsighted! Good and productive lives are lived by people who are enriched by their educations and not just taught how to do this or that. You would give people less than they deserve in the name of practical utility. I offer them a share of their rich cultural inheritance.

How do you react to this debate? Are some subjects of worth, no matter what? Should all schools teach critical thinking and problem-solving skills? How? Is traditional knowledge irrelevant to real-life situations? What should be the main aim of schooling? Is a progressive or a traditional curriculum the best preparation for life?

Workforce School

Maria Ortega's first teaching job was at Elmo High, an inner-city school in a deteriorating neighborhood with a high rate of drug abuse and crime. Whenever she told friends where she worked, they were shocked, felt sorry for her, and some even said they'd rather not teach than have to take a job in a place like that. "But someone has to teach there," Maria would always reply. "How else could the culturally and economically deprived students at Elmo have a chance to get out of the ghetto as I did?"

When Maria began at Elmo, it had been just like many other inner-city schools: a high drop-out rate, drug and discipline problems, a staff with low morale, and students who saw school work as irrelevant to their lives. But then Hector Gomez became principal. He was given a free hand by the Board of Education to develop an experimental curriculum, and things really changed.

Maria was a second-year teacher at Elmo when Mr. Gomez arrived, and she, like the rest of the faculty, was caught up in the spirit of his enterprise to change the school and make a difference in the lives of the students. That was five years ago, and now Maria was reflecting on how much had changed since then.

The local police were seldom called now to break up gang fights or to investigate thefts. The school corridors were clean, and the passings between classes, orderly. Attendance was high; so was staff morale. It didn't seem possible that all this was due to Mr. Gomez's charismatic personality and his decision to make the school a vocational, work-study, community-cooperative school. Mr. Gomez visited and signed up local businesses and small factories to accept students as interns on released work-study assignments. Teachers eagerly took turns visiting students at work sites and finding ways to bring the world of work meaningfully into their classes. After they graduated, many students were finding jobs in the places where they had interned. It seemed like a miracle to Maria!

Then one day a group of students came in to see her at the end of the day. Their spokesperson said, "Mrs. Ortega, can we apply to college with our curriculum at Elmo and become teachers like you? Our guidance counselor told us we don't have enough academic credits."

Have Mr. Gomez's changes provided real opportunities for the students or simply fit them into the system? If you were Maria, what would you tell the students who came to you? Were Mr. Gomez's aims good aims? Should general education aim at transmitting a common culture to all? Would a "two-cultures" form of education perpetuate a two-class society?

Individual Differences and Equality of Opportunity

A: In this land of opportunity, I believe that people, through the agency of education, should be free to grow and develop to the limits of their potential. After all, promoting the good of the individual ultimately serves the good of the society as a whole, doesn't it? Therefore, our schools must find ways to identify and educate the unique talents of each student. We should not waste effort trying to make all people all things. It's not only inefficient, but also unfair, to force someone without musical or scientific talent, for instance, to struggle and compete with those who have a gift in those areas. Wouldn't it be more humane, as well as a greater benefit to society as a whole, to spare the untalented musician or the nonscientifically minded person from required courses in those areas? Let each learn what he or she is best suited for.

B: You make a good case, but I think that it's wrongheaded. How can we decide what people are best suited for? We have to permit people to demonstrate their talents. That can only happen if we give a broad, rich, and full education to all people. We should allow specialization and development of individual talent to proceed only partially in higher education, but most fully in private business, industry, or professional schools. Equal opportunity requires that.

A: No, the point of equal opportunity is to provide an education that will develop everyone's *individual* talents. We have sophisticated tests that can identify human potential of all kinds. While general intelligence tests are our best indicators, we can also distinguish artistic and scientific talent, manual and intellectual skill; we can even test for personality factors that match different personality profiles to potential for success in suitable vocations. Our ability to screen and sort people gets more reliable each year as test makers create and sharpen their diagnostic instruments.

B: But if they are only getting better, are our tests really that good that we can use them to sort out human beings as if they were sheep? Even one mismatch or denial of opportunity for a person to grow in one direction rather than another would be a moral transgression against an individual that might change a whole life. If we can't be absolutely certain, then we shouldn't sort or track students at all. Even if tests were 100 percent reliable, why should they be the criteria for deciding a person's future? Are we so sure that our standards are the right ones? Even reading groups in elementary school are questionable. We label children, and they tend to live up to our expectations, high or low. This could be a self-fulfilling prophecy. We stigmatize those we label as low achievers, and they do not get a fair chance to exceed our expectations. Opportunity means keeping open as many possibilities as possible for each and every student and not closing any.

A: While you're warmhearted, it is unfortunate that you are also mistaken. Opportunity means giving everyone a chance to show potential. But it is we who must measure that potential fairly and put people where they belong, where they will do themselves and society the most good. Why would we have schools if we didn't think children need guidance? It may be difficult, and our methods may be imperfect, but specialized education is the only intelligent, efficient, and fair way to do things in a complex society like ours. Maybe a little general education is needed, but the special talents of individuals are the valuable common property of society. We are morally obligated to identify and train these unique capacities for the benefit of all.

Is specialized education more important than general education in a democratic society? Is there a basic education all citizens should have in common? Is equality of opportunity best served by general or specialized education? Is the ideal of having opportunity best served by keeping possibilities open or by identifying individual talents and nurturing them?

Mass or Class Culture?

A: Everybody complains about school being separate from life, but nobody does anything about it! Students are forced to read Shakespeare when, in real life, no one needs to force them to read comics and racy novels. They're forced to listen to symphonies and opera when, in real life, rock and country music sing to them. Art isn't in museums but all around them in advertising and in the design of useful and beautiful products. Even our modern artists, the soup-can and comic-strip painters, saw that! Why do we persist in trying to initiate students into an artificial, esoteric culture, when their own real culture is so rich and satisfying? Why not help them critically engage their real-world culture and have school make a difference in their lives?

B: Because Shakespeare, Beethoven, and Rembrandt *do* make a difference in the lives of all of us. They represent some of the heights human beings have achieved, and their works speak eloquently to universal human emotions and feelings in ways barely plumbed in the pop culture. Why use mediocre examples to teach aesthetic and humane sensitivity, when models of excellence are there for the taking?

A: Because students won't take them! Because students feel that their art forms are not appreciated by us. In fact, we make them feel as if their genuinely felt appreciation for their literature, art, movies, and music is a low form of uncultured, adolescent emotionalism, a phase one might have to go through but should grow out of. We treat as trivial and meaningless what they take very seriously, as reflecting their deepest emotions and needs.

B: Emotions are not what culture and art forms are about. It is intellect in its highest forms that creates and appreciates culture. The business of the school is developing intellect, not pampering the emotions. Television provides all the emotion, base action, and nonintellectual stimulation students need—and then some. We need to counterbalance such negative cultural forces.

A: Why negative? Why must what speaks to masses of good, hardworking, plain people be negative and what speaks to only a few who see themselves as an elite be positive? Our levels of intellectual ability may differ, but all humans share the same emotional capacities to feel love, anger, empathy, caring, and joy. Our curriculum should capitalize on this capacity and use the common art forms of everyday life to bridge the gap between school and life and teach our youth about the common humanity of all human beings.

B: You win. Let's get rid of all the literature books from the storeroom and library and replace them with comics and drugstore paperbacks in our English courses. Let's clean those old-fashioned instruments and classical records out of the music room and replace them with guitars, electronic sound enhancement, and the lastest pop records. As for art, let's . . .

A: Wait a minute, we don't have to go that far, do we?

What do you think? Does popular culture have a place in the curriculum? Does teaching "high culture" make students feel that their culture is inferior? Is it?

National Reports on Education

A: The new President's Commission on Education has made it clear in its reports that we are falling behind in the production of engineers and basic scientists compared to other modern nations. Our capacity to invent, do research, and provide the basis for high-tech industry is eroding, and we soon will become a second-rate power unless the schools do something about it.

B: But the schools as they now function are part of the problem. They are lax on requirements. Students are given too much freedom and choose easier courses over math and science. We need to tighten standards and go back to requiring three years of math and three of science for high school graduation. We need to make the high school diploma stand for something again.

C: But what about students who aren't academically inclined? Do they have to meet those stiff requirements, too, even though they won't go on to college or become scientists and engineers? That's not fair.

B: Sure it is. Fair is giving everyone a chance to meet the requirements. It's unfair to give everyone the same diploma when some take hard courses and some take all easy ones. A diploma should mean something and mean the same thing for everybody.

A: You're both focusing on the wrong issue. To get needed scientists and engineers, we have to provide incentives and develop accurate testing instruments to screen out the untalented from the talented, not require everybody to take stiff math and science courses. Find and reward the talented with government scholarships in math, science, and engineering, and you'll solve the problem.

C: But is it right to use the schools as instruments of national policy to solve the problems of private industry?

A: Why not? That's what schools are, aren't they, instruments of the state? Whether we use them to produce good citizens or good engineers, it's all the same. The proper function of the schools is to serve society's needs.

C: But what happens when the perceptions of those needs change every few years? Must the schools change overnight? And what about the needs of the individual? Where do they come in?

B: What's good for the nation is good for the individual.

C: Always?

Is it always? Are the schools the instrument of society? Should the curriculum serve perceived social needs, or are there some individual or universal needs that are more important? What function do national reports on education serve?

Go Fly a Kite

The founder and trustees of Duhey Academy have always believed that competition is an important motivator for learning, as well as a central element in the productive lives of mature persons. Many aspects of school life at Duhey reflect this basic belief. One traditional event that the students really enjoy is a yearly contest held between the sixth grade classes to determine the best product of a class project. This year, the announced project was kite making, but for the first time in the history of the school, no winner could be determined; there was a tie! Mr. Whitehead, the headmaster, and the three seventh-grade teachers who served as judges independently rated both the class 6A and 6C kites equally on each of the points agreed upon. The class 6B kite definitely came off second best, but 6A's and 6C's entries were first-rate in all respects. So the judges declared a draw and awarded the prize, a field trip to the Museum of Manned Flight, to both classes. Mr. Whitehead wondered, though, if the educational experiences leading up to the kites produced were of equal value. Even though both products were equal, maybe the teaching/learning processes of producing them were not. He knew that Mr. Mullins in 6A was a perfectionist. He had heard that, when the project was announced, Mr. Mullins had gone to the library to read everything he could about kites. Then, to the consternation of his wife, he had spent every evening in his study designing and building kites and every weekend testing his models behind the fieldhouse. When he finally developed a model that outperformed all the others, he drew up a set of blueprints and brought them to his class.

Mr. Mullins gave each student materials and a copy of the blueprint, along with careful instructions and teaching demonstrations at each step in the process. He made it clear that this was not only a contest between classes but also within 6A itself. To produce the best kite was the order of the day for each of his students. He would grade them on their effort and on their product. When they had all finished, it turned out that Jim's kite narrowly won out over Karen's, in Mr. Mullins's judgment, even though he gave each an A+. Karen's initial disappointment was softened somewhat when she found out that 6A's entry had won them a tie with 6C and a trip to the museum.

But in 6C, Ms. Goody had come at the project quite differently. As soon as she knew what the year's project was to be, she told the class and asked them how they thought they should organize their efforts to win the competition. They all knew that Robert was really good with his hands, so they asked him if he would be "quality control" helper on all the kites they produced. Others volunteered to be designers, color coordinators, supply getters, and fabricators. Before long, five small groups of kite makers formed, with each group working together to produce the best kite they could. Robert put the final touches on each and made them ready for testing outside. The whole class witnessed the tests, and each person rated the kites on the points to be considered by the judges. Ms. Goody tallied the ratings, and 6C's entry was determined and submitted. They were all proud to learn that they had won a trip to the museum.

We haven't mentioned 6B except to say that it lost the contest. That is because Mr. Brayne didn't believe in "fads and frills." Oh, he would see to it that he met the letter of the law, and his class would have a kite for the contest, of course. Each student would be given a homework assignment to make a kite, and then he would draw a name out of the hat to see whose kite would be submitted to represent 6B. That would not take much precious class time, he figured, and so he could continue with the history unit on technology that interestingly enough treated human attempts to overcome the force of gravity through the ages. The students seemed to like the unit. It challenged their minds. Their only regret was that they wouldn't be going to the museum. They thought they would get more out of the trip than those who were going.

These three teachers created and taught a different curriculum for the same project. Try to specify each teacher's general aim. Which one best follows the philosophy of the school? Should a teacher try to do so? Was one of these learning experiences better than the others? Why?

Individualized Learning

Bob was a first-year teacher in a first-grade open classroom. Like all the other teachers of his teaching team, Bob had responsibility for one homogeneously grouped math class. The math program of the school was designed as follows: each student progressed through a series of worksheets; when one worksheet was finished correctly, the student went on to the next. In this way, skills in addition, subtraction, multiplication, and other areas were to be learned at an individual's own pace. The idea was that the teacher could give individual attention to those children who needed it. Bob thought that this system made sense. He liked the individualized nature of the program. The students seemed to like the class, too. They were rewarded by the evidence of their progress and by the praise Bob gave when papers were completed.

Before long, though, Bob began to be uneasy about the direction his math class was taking. He felt that he was not really teaching his students. They were just doing worksheets on their own. He had thought he would be able to work one-on-one with the children. Instead, he found he spent almost no time with anyone. There was constantly a line of five or six children either waiting to ask questions or waiting to have papers checked. Bob felt that he could not afford to give as much time to each child as he would have liked, since it would be unfair to keep all the others waiting. The children who finished papers were congratulated and sent on to the next worksheet. The students who had questions were told to try and work out an answer by themselves. They often would, but this usually took the form of three or four unsuccessful guesses before they stumbled upon the correct answer. Furthermore, Bob was so busy at his desk that he had difficulty being sure students were working and behaving as they should. Some students seemed to be progressing much too slowly. Bob was concerned that this was because he had not watched these pupils closely enough. In short, Bob came to see himself less as a teacher and more as a paper pusher.

Bob's worst fears seemed to be realized when one day he held an addition game. Bob chose problems that all the students should have been able to answer, since they came from worksheets all the students had completed. Contrary to Bob's expectations, many of his students were unable to do the problems he chose. It appeared that, indeed, many of Bob's students were not learning.

How would you characterize this conceptualization of math learning? What are its positive features? What went wrong with it? Are there other conceptualizations that might work better for Bob? Was Bob teaching?

Grading Policies

David Levine is the principal of Henry Hudson High School, a large metropolitan secondary school. Because of the size of the student population, several sections of certain courses are offered each year, and each is taught by a different instructor. In the case of modern American history, three teachers offer courses. Students are assigned to these courses according to a simple alphabetical rotation. This simple system has become a complex problem for Mr. Levine.

The first section is taught by Albert Foley. Mr. Foley is a young, somewhat idealistic teacher who believes that stimulating learning experiences form the core of an education. He relies upon the study of current events from newspapers and television, and he encourages his students to initiate independent study projects. Mr. Foley is not as much concerned about command of exact facts as he is about the personal significance that modern American history may come to hold for his students. In that direction, he believes, lies the promise of good citizenship. Students are graded on the basis of essays about topics students themselves select and journals of personal responses to classroom discussions and current events. Among the students, he is known as "Easy A" Foley. In a typical year, 30 percent of his students will receive As, and another 30 percent will receive Bs. The rest are given Cs, with an occasional D for "serious" cases. Mr. Foley says that a student will pass his class if he is able to find his way to the classroom. In his opinion, it is hard enough being a teenager, and he is not going to make it any tougher. He believes that his students really learn and grow in their sense of self-worth because of his policy.

"The facts and nothing but the facts" might be the motto of Mr. William Sampson, the teacher of the second section, for he believes that subject matter is all important. Mr. Sampson relies on the textbook exclusively, and he delivers very detailed lectures. He demands that his students know the facts about American government and recent historical events, and he has very little patience with uninformed opinion. In his view, good citizenship must rest upon a solid foundation of knowledge. He tells his students that they must learn American history backwards and forwards to pass his course. In order to guarantee this, the students must take rigorous objective examinations that test their knowledge of the most exact matters of fact. In a recent class of forty students, the grades were distributed in the following manner: three As, five Bs, eighteen Cs, nine Ds, and five Fs. Mr. Sampson contends that his tests are fair measures of his students' knowledge. The students call him "Slasher Sampson."

Nancy Wright, the teacher of the third section, believes that life is a competition for finite resources, and her course is run in a manner that reflects that belief. In the future, her students will have to struggle for pieces of the pie at the table of life. Similarly, in her classroom they must compete among themselves for places in a hierarchy of achievement. Ms. Wright grades according to a curve. In her most recent group of forty students, there were five As, ten Bs, fifteen Cs, seven Ds, and three Fs, a distribution of grades that she has come to favor after some experience. Ms. Wright uses both essays and objective tests in order to provide some unbiased basis for her judgments. She believes that her proportional approach to grading avoids questions of favoritism and accurately reflects the performance of each student as it compares to those of others in the class. Ms. Wright's students have no nickname for her.

Does the existence of three radically different conceptions of curriculum phenomena produce different curricula under the same course title? Will they all meet the goal of learning history? Is this situation fair to the students?

A Social Studies Curriculum

A: Thank you for coming. As you know, our task is to design an integrated social studies curriculum in global studies for K-12. We will probably have to meet all term. There's a lot of work to do. Where shall we begin?

B: I think we need to agree in general about what form our final product will take. Then we'll know what we're aiming at and have some idea of what we need to do.

A: Good idea! I see by your nodding heads that you all agree with *B*. OK. Let's try to get conceptual closure quickly so we can get down to work. Who will start us off?

C: The most useful thing for the system's teachers and principals would be for us to provide them with a clear and full outline of topics to be covered at each grade level in each school. Then they'd know what to do.

D: That would help, but the curriculum is more than just content. We need to provide teachers with a list of objectives stated in terms of the learning outcomes students are expected to reach. Then they'd know what they were aiming at.

E: No, lists of objectives are just useless bureaucratic formulas. Teachers don't pay attention to them. They know that what really counts is what the students actually do. We need to provide teachers with descriptions of class and individual student activities that can be engaged in to provide mastery of the content prescribed for each grade level.

B: I like what you've all said, but let's think about it. Isn't the essence of a curriculum what a student experiences—not activities, not objectives, not content. If we could only describe the kind of educative experiences of human and global significance we want our students to have, then teachers would have a real conception of what our new curriculum is about.

A: And I thought we'd get quick closure!

Do you think these disagreements are really fundamental, or are they merely matters of terminology or minor matters of personal preference? Does the lack of agreement arise from estimates of what will be most helpful to teachers implementing the new curriculum? To the kind of learning students will achieve? Do you think the committee can function with these different conceptions of what curriculum really is? If not, how would you, if you were *A*, begin to reconcile or overcome these differences?

To Each His Own

A: Our national tradition of local control of schooling isn't meant just to give everybody a say in education; it also gives people a chance to adapt their school's curriculum and aims to local conditions. If you're in a large city with a heavy immigration of non-English-speaking families, a bilingual curriculum becomes a must. If you're in a stable, single-language, rural community, it might be new modes of computerized agricultural bookkeeping or importing cultural arts groups that makes sense in your curriculum. To allow people to set their own objectives and form their own curricula is not only rational but democratic.

B: That sounds good, but doesn't that invite educational chaos? Anything goes? To each his own? Aren't there some basic objectives, some subjects and values all schools ought to serve in a democratic society, regardless of local conditions? Shouldn't we strive to find and agree on some national objectives like literacy, good citizenship, preparation for meaningful work? Shouldn't all students study math, science, history, literature? Isn't providing equality of educational opportunity an important principle to follow in all curriculum making in a democracy?

A: Yes, but in a democracy you can't force those things on people. You have to trust the people to decide on such things for themselves. What we as educators can do is provide the framework to guide the process rationally and ensure that it will be done thoroughly and efficiently. Then it's up to each community, each school, and each teacher to decide on specifics.

B: At first you sounded like a realist saying we must take local conditions into account, and now you've become an idealist, not paying any attention to reality at all! Teachers and communities don't really decide. The federal government legislates and enforces equality of educational opportunity in public schools; state legislatures and state departments of education require and prescribe all sorts of curricula from driver education and civics to the subjects needed for high school graduation. There is more *required* commonality in the curricula of our schools than your way of thinking about curriculum development would lead us to expect. How do you explain that?

A: Similar conditions and similarly perceived problems produce similar solutions. The key is to make the steps in the process clear, so people will see that their objectives come out of their perceived needs and can only be met by a careful selection, organization, and evaluation of relevant educational activities.

B: But if you want people to be free to choose, why must they choose your procedures for curriculum making?

A: They're the only rational procedures available.

Do you agree with A's last comment? Should curriculum determination be entirely a local affair, or should larger social and political units be allowed to decide basic curriculum matters? Is local control a myth or a reality? Can there be a value-free procedure for curriculum making?

The Geometry Curriculum

Edgar Ortiz had agreed to take over the geometry sections at Metropolitan High School when Etta Foote retired. In his previous two years at Metropolitan, Edgar had taught second-year algebra and calculus, but Etta's retirement necessitated some reshuffling of class assignments. Edgar volunteered to take the geometry classes; he was looking forward to the change.

Now he was looking through the text, trying to develop an outline for his lesson plans for the year. Edgar had never taught geometry before (and neither had any of Edgar's colleagues, which explains their joy when Edgar volunteered). It had been a number of years since he had taken a geometry course, too. So Edgar was relying on the plan suggested in the teacher's edition of the text. Edgar had nearly finished when a thought occurred to him. He remembered how his high school geometry teacher had spent much time on elementary logic. Not only had the exercises been fun, but the practice they gave had benefited Edgar considerably when the lessons on geometric proofs were encountered.

This textbook, though, did not contain any such material. Edgar looked back at his outline. The material in the book was extensive enough to fill the whole school year, with some left over more than likely. Edgar could not see any material that was irrelevant; and because he did not consider himself an expert in geometry, he was uncomfortable with the thought of eliminating something.

But Edgar also remembered that his aim was to help students learn mathematics, and he knew that his training in logic had been a big help to him throughout his career in mathematics. What's more, he had always been concerned to keep his classes flexible and interesting: Should he give that up now by adhering strictly to a textbook's curriculum?

Edgar leaned back from his desk. He had decided that he really was not satisfied with the text. But what was he going to do? As a beginning teacher, Edgar did not have a library of alternative resources at hand. To develop his own curriculum would take a lot of work, more work than he would have time for. He was not even really sure what it was he *should* teach in the geometry class. Edgar was in a bind. He knew the text wasn't adequate for the aims he had in mind. On the other hand, the text provided his only comprehensive guide to what should be taught. What can Edgar do?

The assumption usually is that one's objectives determine the curriculum. But Edgar's case raises another possibility: To what extent do curriculum materials determine, consciously or not, the aims of the teacher?

Does it matter? To what extent is the Tyler rationale appropriate for a teacher to use in thinking about a new subject?

Do Procedures Make a Difference?

The Amana School District appointed a ten-person committee to develop a revised curriculum in social studies for the elementary grades. The superintendent had charged the group to follow sound principles of curriculum making in order to develop the best possible program of studies. She had also said she hoped the committee would give a great deal of attention in their curriculum to global studies. She felt that "our globe is shrinking, yet our children are all too ignorant of other lands and peoples."

The committee chair, Anzel Familoff, was social studies coordinator for the district. He believed that Tyler's ideas were the soundest, most professionally accepted way for the committee to carry out its charge, so he outlined a four-step process for their summer's work: state objectives, select learning activities, organize learning activities, and develop means of evaluation.

Just as he was about to describe to the committee how they would go about stating their objectives, he was interrupted by Sadie Hill, a respected, outspoken senior teacher on the committee. "Anzel," she said, "Tyler's method is mechanistic. It reflects the technological bias of modern industrial society. I believe, and our district philosophy backs me up, that our main duty as educators is to help each child develop to the fullest, and I don't see how we can do that if we build their curriculum using this mechanistic, uniform, lock-step, behavioristic model."

Dr. Familoff was taken aback by this unexpected criticism but defended Tyler vigorously. "Tyler's method is completely neutral," he said. "You can be as humane as you like in any and all of the four steps. Tyler does not tell you what objectives you should pursue; he leaves it up to you. You just follow sound rational procedures and use your own philosophy of education to determine your objectives."

In the debate that followed, several members of the committee expressed misgivings about Tyler's rationale, agreeing with Ms. Hill that it seemed mechanistic, technological, and inhumane. They agreed that it seemed to treat all goals alike, but they insisted that some goals are difficult, if not impossible, to state and that pursuing only those you could state neglected some of the most important, but subtle, educational goals—such as becoming a good person or achieving a good self-image. Others agreed with Dr. Familoff and urged the dissidents to accept the

Tyler framework to try to objectify the goals they espoused and get on with the work.

Whose side would you be on? How do you justify your stand?

If you were the district curriculum coordinator who stopped by to discover the committee deeply divided over how to proceed, what would you do? Would you try to resolve the disagreement? If so, what arguments would you use to convince each side? Would you see a way to proceed in spite of this disagreement? If so, how would you avoid continuing controversy?

Was the superintendent's suggestion to emphasize global studies legitimate in terms of Tyler's rationale? Should the committee, assuming they decide to follow Tyler's rationale, accept the superintendent's suggestions? Why, or why not?

Teaching "Relevant" Literature

Today had been a big day for Jennifer Calhoun. For the first time as a student teacher, she had taken over the junior literature classes in which she had been observing. Jennifer had put a great deal of thought into the unit on twentieth-century American literature she was to teach for the next six weeks. The progressive theorists she had been reading about in her foundations course at State College had greatly influenced her thinking, so she aimed to make the students themselves the center of her unit. She was not so concerned that the students learn to analyze literature; she wanted them to be excited by their work, enjoy their readings, and take away something meaningful from the class. In Jennifer's opinion, these things had not happened in the class up to that time.

So Jennifer spent a great deal of time developing a reading list that would be appealing and relevant to the students. She chose stories, poems, and books about teenagers; some were even written by young people. Because the student population was diverse, she chose works by authors of different ethnic and racial backgrounds. The activities she developed concentrated on free discussion and creative writing assignments. She really wanted them to learn to like literature and structured her curriculum accordingly.

Armed with her enthusiasm and thoughtfully developed plan for meeting her goals, Jennifer introduced her unit to the classes (and to her supervisor, who was observing that day). But contrary to her expectations, the students did not seem to be particularly excited by the readings and plans she presented. Some even objected to them.

This afternoon, when discussing the day with her supervisor, Jennifer frankly admitted that she was puzzled and dejected by the students' reactions. The advice her supervisor offered puzzled Jennifer even more. Her supervisor told her that by this time students were pretty set in their ways and perceived new approaches as threatening. Also, in this junior class, many students were looking to apply to colleges. They knew that PSATs, SATs, and achievement tests were right around the corner and that standard questions on the literature sections would not be about the books on Jennifer's list. The supervisor advised Jennifer to return to the standard curriculum and standard assignments and tests. It was only fair to her students not to change things.

What would you do if you were Jennifer? Should procedures for curriculum making include facing situational realities? Is innovation impossible? Were Jennifer's procedure more like Tyler's, Schwab's, or Freire's? How would you proceed to develop a literature unit in this situation?

The Teacher as Critic

Madelyn Harris was proverbially caught between a rock and a hard place. She was just completing her first year of teaching in her first job, a position at Fulton High. One week ago, her principal, John Wheelwright, had taken to the superintendent and the Board of Education a plan for instituting a program of minimum competencies and behavioral objectives for the curriculum at Fulton. This plan had been well received. John had cited national reports on education and statistics on declining grades at Fulton to demonstrate the need for curriculum reform. He had distributed excerpts from research studies that attested to the success of schools that had minimum competency standards. John had been persuasive. The board decided to consider the proposal and take a vote on it at their next meeting, which was now three weeks away.

In the past week, there had been controversy at Fulton. For various reasons, some of the faculty were not at all in accord with John's plan. Of these, some had decided that they would have to go along anyway, either because they believed it was the community's right to decide or because they felt the matter had been essentially decided already. But the remainder of the group, though a minority of the faculty, were vociferous in their protests. Their leader, Alex Thomassetti, was trying to rally a bloc of teachers to present a rebuttal to John's proposal at the next meeting. Alex had been pressuring Madelyn to join his group. Madelyn was also getting pressure from John. He had let it be known that he wanted a faculty at Fulton that could work together with him. In other words, untenured teachers (such as Madelyn) would not be offered contracts if they opposed his program.

Madelyn looked through the material John had shown the board. It was persuasive. And there seemed to be merit in the task of improving student performance. But the behavioral-objectives approach did not fit in well with Madelyn's philosophy of teaching. She went back to some texts she had used in college to look for material about this issue to help her put her misgivings into more concrete form. She found she sympathized a great deal with interpretivist and humanistic writers. Because they viewed knowledge as a function of culture and of group interactions, they object-ed to the view that rigid educational goals should be imposed upon the classroom by external authority.

However, Madelyn could find few suggestions for alternatives to John's plan. If that approach was wrong, what was one to do instead? Madelyn read and thought enough to find problems with John's plan, but the more she studied the more she felt that having a complete grasp of all the issues was beyond her.

Madelyn told Alex of her research. He said that he would use anything she found as ammunition against John. But Madelyn objected to this use of research evidence as projectiles in a political war. She began to wonder whether the issue was what was the best educational program—or if it was based on a struggle for personal power between John and Alex.

She told Alex that she would present her research to the board, but as a professional educator concerned to investigate all aspects of the issue. Alex scoffed. He said that Madelyn was naive to think that research facts were at issue. It was simply a case of them against us, Alex said. No matter how objective Madelyn would try to appear, she would be per-ceived as an opponent by John and the board. If Madelyn really believed in her position, Alex said, she could not remain objective; she would have to join his group.

What should Madelyn do? Who benefits from criticism? Under what conditions can criticism be persuasive, and to what extent? To what de-gree must one have all the answers in order to advocate a position or present an argument? Should one advocate a position? Is it possible to remain neutral?

Theory and Practice

A: These professors sure make theory sound good, but it's really not much use to people who work in real schools. Oh, once in a while a research finding will come out that's useful, but for the most part it's just ivory-tower, armchair talk.

B: And even when some finding is useful, like in the "time-on-task" research, it's just a commonsense finding that most teachers have been using anyway. It shouldn't take a million-dollar research program to find out that the more time a student spends on a learning task, the better the chance of his or her learning it!

C: At least the research that deals with classrooms and teachers has some potential for usefulness, but that history and philosophy and critical stuff is just too far removed from reality ever to make a difference in a school or classroom.

D: You all seem to consider "usefulness" to be a very "direct" idea. You seem to believe that if something in educational scholarship and research doesn't directly tell you what to do or *how* to do it, then it's not useful or worthwhile. I happen to think (and not just because I'm a professor) that knowledge can serve other important functions besides telling us *how* to do things. It can create in us an awareness of things we might not otherwise see and force us to reflect on the justice of the system we are a part of. It can give us historical perspective so we don't have to reinvent the wheel every time and so we can project ideas about our teaching, the school, and the curriculum into the future. It can help us see what sorts of things might be wrong with our current practices and can give us a kind of broad professional perspective on things that makes us more than mere technicians in the factories of education. It can . . .

A: There he goes again!

B: He sure is a professor!

C: Talk about being removed from everyday life! Factories of education! We were taught that they were citadels of learning!

A: See, all that theoretical stuff we were taught doesn't connect with practice at all. I can be a good teacher and a real professional without any of that irrelevant stuff.

Do you agree or disagree with *D*? Are there different ways that scholarship and research in education can relate to educational practice? Should curriculum and classroom research aim to tell practitioners "how to do it"? Can you think of one thing you've learned in this book that will make a difference in you as a teacher, or has it all been "ivory tower"?

One School's Philosophy of Education

WE BELIEVE

That our school exists so that all may learn

That in our complex, modern world, a broad diversity of knowledge, skills, values, and attitudes is essential

That it is our duty to create a rich environment in which all can learn to
—effectively use verbal and written modes of communication
—think critically and logically
—master basic computational skills
—maintain one's health
—appreciate our artistic and cultural values
—understand the sciences and their effects on us and the world
—form productive life plans and develop useful general vocational skills and attitudes
—act morally and responsibly as a member of our community
—discharge one's duties as a citizen in a democratic society
—use good judgment as consumers, adults, and citizens
—develop the ability to continue to learn and grow as a productive human being.

Would you disagree with or remove any of the commitments and aims from this list? Would you add any? Which two or three would you rank highest in priority and which two or three lowest? Compare your rankings with the rankings of other students in your class. Do you think your differences, if any, can be resolved? Do you think the differences, if any, need to be resolved? Would such a statement of school philosophy be helpful in curriculum planning? To what extent is it essential for a teacher to agree with the philosophy of the school in which he or she teaches?

Whose Aims Matter?

Webster Academy, a private nonsectarian college preparatory school, was founded in 1872 for the purpose of "instilling gentlemanly virtues and a knowledge of the liberal arts." Through most of its history the school has offered a traditional curriculum, including Latin, English literature, and rhetoric, and it has been noted for its discipline and academic rigor. Webster Academy has enjoyed a good reputation, as most of its graduates have attended prestigious colleges.

In recent years, under the leadership of the latest headmaster, Donald Hearns, the character and curriculum of Webster Academy have undergone significant changes. Mr. Hearns, an alumnus, was selected as one who could guide the school during a period of change, yet remain in touch with its tradition. In 1971, under pressure from some alumni and because of the need to broaden its tuition base, the school became a coeducational institution. At that time, Mr. Hearns argued that a truly liberal education requires exposure to a variety of experiences and that coeducation was one of the more interesting experiences. Since then, an extensive program of girls' athletics has been developed, and some courses in feminist studies have been added to the curriculum.

During that same period, the concerns of a more activist generation of students placed further demands upon the school and the leadership of Mr. Hearns. Student request and some protest caused Webster to relax some regulations of dress and behavior, and the students were granted greater personal freedom. These students also wanted an education that was more relevant to their present experience and concerns, and the academy's curriculum was altered in accord with their wishes. Courses on such subjects as marriage, ecology, and futurism were introduced. The school continued to chart its course through the changing tastes of its clientele.

Recently, the students and their parents have turned to more pragmatic concerns. The pressures and worries of changed economic circumstances have engendered an interest in a more career-oriented education. This new generation of students expects the school to prepare them for commercial success in perilous economic times. The Parental Support Association, a group that has been very generous in the past, has formally requested that the school offer courses in computer science, personal finance, and career strategy. They contend that Webster Academy must continue to be an institution that mirrors the needs and interests of modern times.

This request, and its implications for the identity and curriculum integrity of Webster Academy, has brought about a spiritual crisis at the school. Certain alumni and older faculty have charged that acceptance of these latest proposals will be proof that Webster Academy has lost sight of its educational mission and has abandoned its legitimate authority to the whims of adolescents and nervous parents. Where once existed a unified, disciplined program of general education, these critics now see a "cafeteria-style" system in which immature students pick and choose from a body of unrelated, undemanding courses. As a result, they believe that the students are being miseducated and culturally impoverished. Declining SAT scores are cited as evidence for this contention. They also charge that the school has abandoned responsibility for moral education and character development. Theft and drug use, heretofore unknown at the school, have become serious problems. They believe that today's Webster Academy student is slovenly, uncouth, and immoral, a disgrace to a proud institution.

These alumni and faculty demand that the misguided "pop" approach to education be abandoned. They have proposed reforms in which the elective system would be curtailed and some modernistic courses would be dropped from the curriculum. They jointly recommend a reinstitution of a unified curriculum that emphasizes traditional studies and a return to an educational philosophy and corresponding disciplinary policy that espouse civilized virtues and norms of proper conduct. They have asked Mr. Hearns to exert his leadership in this matter.

Mr. Hearns intends to do so, but he is not sure what his leadership entails. He has reflected upon his role as an educator and upon the mission of the school.

What would you do if you were Mr. Hearns? Whose aims should count? Those of the alumni? Of the students? Of the parents? Of society? Of the headmaster? Should the school aim to transmit the "higher culture" or mirror society or allow students to fulfill perceived needs? Is there a curriculum that can reconcile the several viewpoints? Should a curriculum necessarily seek to reconcile such conflicts?

Notes

Chapter 2

1. John Dewey, *Democracy and Education* (New York: Macmillan, 1916), p. 107.

2. R. S. Peters, *Authority, Responsibility and Education* (London: George Allen and Unwin, 1959), ch. 7.

3. Jean Jacques Rousseau, *Emile* (London: J. M. Dent and Sons, 1911), p. 1.

4. Jean Jacques Rousseau, *The Social Contract and Discourses* (New York: E. P. Dutton, 1914), p. 5.

5. He also included a section on "Sophie," about the proper education of a girl in a prefeminist era.

6. Lawrence A. Cremin, *The Transformation of the School* (New York: Vintage Books, 1961).

7. Harold Rugg, ed., *The Twenty-Sixth Yearbook of the National Society for the Study of Education*: Part I, "Curriculum Making Past and Present"; Part II, "Foundations of Curriculum Making" (Bloomington, Ind.: Public School Publishing Co., 1927).

8. All subsequent references in this chapter are to author and pages in Part II of the *Yearbook*.

9. William H. Kilpatrick, "Statement of Position," II: 121.

10. Ibid., p. 132.

11. Charles H. Judd, "Supplementary Statement," II: 113.

12. Harold Rugg, "Curriculum Making: Points of Emphasis," II: 149.

13. W. C. Bagley, "Supplementary Statement," II: 29–40.

14. Kilpatrick, "Statement of Position," II: 122.

15. Composite Statement of the Society's Committee on Curriculum-Making, "The Foundations of Curriculum Making," II: 17.

16. Ibid., pp. 18–19.

17. Judd, "Supplementary Statement," II: 114–16.

18. Kilpatrick, "Statement of Position," II: 131.

Chapter 3

1. *Report of the Committee of Ten on Secondary School Studies* (Washington, D.C.: National Education Association, 1896).

2. *Cardinal Principles of Secondary Education* (Washington, D.C.: U.S. Bureau of Education, Bulletin No. 35, 1918), pp. 10–11.

3. The Harvard Committee, *General Education in a Free Society* (Cambridge, Mass.: Harvard University Press, 1945), pp. 4, 5, 9.

4. Ibid., pp. 64–65, emphasis in original.

5. Ibid., p. 54.

6. G. H. Bantock, *Culture, Industrialisation and Education* (London: Routledge and Kegan Paul, 1968); idem, *Dilemmas of the Curriculum* (New York: John Wiley and Sons, 1980).

7. Bantock, *Culture, Industrialisation and Education*, p. 65.

8. Ibid., p. 71

Chapter 4

1. Gilbert Ryle, *The Concept of Mind* (New York: Barnes and Noble, 1949).

2. Harry S. Broudy, B. Othanel Smith, and Joe R. Burnett, *Democracy and Excellence in American Secondary Education* (Chicago: Rand McNally, 1963), ch. 3 passim. We have taken some liberties with their discussion of these uses of school learning to fit our purposes in this chapter.

3. Benjamin S. Bloom, J. Thomas Hastings, and George F. Madaus, *Taxonomy of Educational Objectives: Handbook I, The Cognitive Domain* (New York: David McKay, 1956).

4. Alfred North Whitehead, *The Aims of Education* (New York: Macmillan, 1929), ch. 2.

5. John Dewey, *The Child and the Curriculum* (Chicago: University of Chicago Press, 1902).

6. Jerome Bruner, *On Knowing* (Cambridge, Mass.: Harvard University Press, 1962), p. 126.

7. Jerome Bruner, *The Process of Education* (Cambridge, Mass.: Harvard University Press, 1963), p. 12.

8. William H. Kilpatrick, "The Project Method," *Teachers College Record* 19 (September 1918): 319–35.

9. John Dewey, *Democracy and Education* (New York: Macmillan, 1916), chs. 16–17.

10. Paul Hirst, *Knowledge and the Curriculum* (London: Routledge and Kegan Paul, 1974).

11. Jerome Bruner, *Man: A Course of Study* (Washington, D.C.: Curriculum Development Associates, 1970).

12. William H. Kilpatrick, *Philosophy of Education* (New York: Macmillan, 1951), ch. 23.

Chapter 5

1. Harold Rugg, "Three Decades of Mental Discipline: Curriculum Making via National Committees," in Part I, "Curriculum Making Past and Present," *The Twenty-Sixth Yearbook of the National Society for the Study of Education*, ed. Harold Rugg (Bloomington, Ind.: Public School Publishing Co., 1927), pp. 48–49.

2. Franklin Bobbitt, *How to Make a Curriculum* (New York: Houghton Mifflin, 1924).

3. Daniel Tanner and Laurel Tanner, *Curriculum Development*, 2nd ed. (New York: Macmillan, 1980), ch. 3.

4. Ralph W. Tyler, *Basic Principles of Curriculum and Instruction* (Chicago: University of Chicago Press, 1949), p. 1.

5. Ibid., pp. 1–2.

6. Ibid., p, 53.

7. W. James Popham, *The Teacher-Empiricist* (Los Angeles: Tinnon-Brown, 1970).

8. Ibid., pp. 21–27.

9. Joseph J. Schwab, *The Practical: A Language for Curriculum* (Washington, D.C.: National Education Association, 1970), p. 38.

10. Ibid., p. 1, emphasis in original.

11. Ibid., p. 2.

12. Decker Walker, "The Process of Curriculum Development: A Naturalistic Model," *School Review* 80 (November 1971): 51–65.

13. Paulo Freire, *Pedagogy of the Oppressed* (New York: Herder and Herder, 1970).

14. Ibid., p. 52.

15. Ibid., p. 66.

16. John I. Goodlad and Maurice N. Richter, Jr., *The Development of a Conceptual System for Dealing with Problems of Curriculum and Instruction* (Washington, D.C.: The Cooperative Research Program of the Office of Education, 1966).

Chapter 6

1. The National Commission on Excellence in Education, *A Nation at Risk: The Imperative for Education Reform* (Washington, D.C.: U.S. Department of Education, 1983); and Ernest Boyer, *High School: A Report on Secondary Education in America* (Princeton, N.J.: Carnegie Foundation for the Advancement of Teaching, 1983).

2. Herbert Kliebard, "The Tyler Rationale," *School Review* 78 (February 1970): 259–72.

3. Ibid., p. 270.

4. Michael Apple, *Ideology and Curriculum* (London: Routledge and Kegan Paul, 1979).

5. Ibid., p. 53.

6. U. Dahllöf, *Ability Groupings, Content Validity and Curriculum Process Analysis* (New York: Teachers College Press, 1971).

7. Ibid., p. 79.

8. Walter Ong, *Rhetoric, Romance, and Technology* (Ithaca, N.Y.: Cornell University Press, 1971).

9. Ibid., p. 264.

10. Ibid., p. 275.

11. Ibid., pp. 277–78.

Chapter 7

1. Jürgen Habermas, *Knowledge and Human Interests*, trans. Jeremy J. Shapiro (Boston: Beacon Press, 1971). Habermas also contrasts human "technical interests" in problem solving with our "practical interests" in living together in a satisfactory manner and with our "emancipatory interests" in our own freedom and the freedom of others.

2. Stanley M. Elam, *The Gallup Poll of Attitudes Toward Education, 1969–1973* (Bloomington, Ind.: Phi Delta Kappa, 1973), p. 123.

3. Ibid., p. 125.

4. Alec Gallup, "Teachers Attitudes Toward the Public Schools, Part 2," *Phi Delta Kappan* 66 (January 1985): 327.

5. Ibid., p. 327.

6. D. J. O'Connor, *An Introduction to the Philosophy of Education* (London: Routledge and Kegan Paul, 1957), p. 17.

Annotated Bibliography

Adler, Mortimer. *The Paideia Proposal*. New York: Macmillan, 1982.
> A radical proposal from a classical philosopher to dedicate America's schools to a curriculum that is the same for all and emphasizes classic intellectual aims.

Apple, Michael, *Teachers and Texts*. New York: Routledge and Kegan Paul, 1986.
> Urges teachers to critically reflect on political, economic, and cultural forces and relations of class, gender, and race that have shaped education and the curriculum.

Ben-Peretz, Miriam. *The Teacher-Curriculum Encounter*. Albany: State University of New York Press, 1990.
> This book addresses the need for more professional and creative use of curriculum materials, and heightened teacher involvement in the process.

Bloom, Benjamin. *All Our Children Learning*. New York: McGraw-Hill, 1981.
> An impassioned statement from the originator of Mastery Learning. A balanced combination of scientific and moral concerns and procedures.

Bowers, C. A., and Flinders, David J. *Responsive Teaching*. New York: Teachers College Press, 1990.
> Provides a conceptual basis for treating the classroom as an ecology of linguistic and cultural patterns that should be taken into account as part of the teacher's curriculum decision making.

Connelly, F. Michael, and Clandinin, D. Jean. *Teachers as Curriculum Planners*. New York: Teachers College Press, 1988.
> A how-to book, a guide to understanding classroom life for teachers who take their own curriculum work seriously.

Counts, George S. *Dare the School Build a New Social Order?* New York: John Day Co., 1932.
> A classic call-to-arms for social reformers who would use the schools as a means to broader social reforms.

Cremin, Lawrence A. *The Transformation of the School*. New York: Vintage Books, 1961.
> A history of America's most extensive educational reform effort, progressive education. Essential to understanding the distinctive American pattern of educational practice.

Dewey, John. *Democracy and Education*. New York: Macmillan, 1916.
   The most comprehensive and influential book by America's most profound and influential educational theorist.
Eisner, Elliot W. *The Educational Imagination* (2nd ed.). New York: Macmillan, 1987.
   A comprehensive treatment of curriculum issues from a writer who draws his inspiration from the arts.
Freire, Paulo. *Pedagogy of the Oppressed*. New York: Herder and Herder, 1970.
   Advocates a form of education for raising the consciousness of the oppressed.
Hirst, Paul. *Knowledge and the Curriculum*. London: Routledge and Kegan Paul, 1974.
   A contemporary British philosopher who uses the concept of forms of knowledge to explicate the educational aim of developing the mind. Advocates the priority of intellectual aims in general education.
Kliebard, Herbert. *The Struggle for the American Curriculum 1893–1958*. London: Routledge and Kegan Paul, 1987.
   A history of curriculum reform in twentieth-century America.
Murphy, Joseph, ed. *The Educational Reform Movement of the 1980s*. Berkeley, CA: McCutchan, 1990.
   Informative readings on the most recent series of curriculum reform movements, those involving action by the states to improve their education systems.
Oakes, Jeannie. *Keeping Track: How Schools Structure Inequality*. New Haven: Yale University Press, 1985.
   An analysis of how some schools organize their curriculum so as to provide unequal educational opportunities to students of different races and socioeconomic groups.
Phenix, Philip. *Realms of Meaning*. New York: McGraw-Hill, 1964.
   A thoughtful attempt to present the practical plan of a curriculum conceived through the ways various disciplinary modes of thinking act and interact to give meaning to human experience.
Rousseau, Jean Jacques. *Emile*. London: J. M. Dent and Sons, 1911.
   Classic statement of naturalism in education that has profoundly influenced contemporary Western ideas and practices.
Schwab, Joseph. *Science, Curriculum and Liberal Education*. Chicago: University of Chicago Press, 1978.
   Collected writings of a philosopher and educator who builds upon Deweyan ideas to develop a balanced contemporary approach to general education. Also see *The Practical: A Language for Curriculum* (Washington, DC.: National Education Association, 1970).
Sizer, Theodore. *Horace's Compromise*. Boston: Houghton Mifflin, 1984.
   The composite picture of Horace, a dedicated teacher, whose ideals are compromised by the conditions in which he must work. A plea for secondary school reform.
Stodolsky, Susan. *The Subject Matters*. Chicago: University of Chicago Press, 1988.
   Analyzes studies of elementary school classrooms to show that teachers teach differently when they teach different subjects.
Taba, Hilda. *Curriculum Development: Theory and Practice*. New York: Harcourt Brace Jovanovich, 1960.

A big, sprawling book by one of the most talented practitioners of collaborative curriculum work between universities and schools.

Tyler, Ralph. *Basic Principles of Curriculum and Instruction*. Chicago: University of Chicago Press, 1949.

The classic work of modern curriculum theory. Must reading for anyone who would understand subsequent writing in this field.

Vandenberg, Donald. *Education as a Human Right*. New York: Teachers College Press, 1990.

Accepting cultural pluralism and multiple intelligence as facts of life, Vandenberg argues nevertheless that there is a core of knowledge for all to learn as their human right.

Walker, Decker F. *Fundamentals of Curriculum*. San Diego, CA: Harcourt Brace Jovanovich, 1990.

A comprehensive textbook incorporating a view of curriculum as a practical endeavor and suggesting how this perspective can lead to improvements in the classroom curriculum, the school curriculum, and in large-scale curriculum policy.

Whitehead, Alfred North. *The Aims of Education*. New York: Macmillan, 1929.

Argues for broad, liberal education emphasizing fundamental scholarly disciplines and against inert ideas and empty formalism.

Index